Suburban
LEGENDS

LIBRARY OF CONGRESS CATALOGING IN PUBLICATION NUMBER:
2006922745

ISBN-10: 1-59474-051-8
ISBN-13: 978-1-59474-051-0

PRINTED IN CHINA
TYPESET IN MATRIX

DESIGNED BY BRYN ASHBURN
ILLUSTRATIONS BY MELISSA GRIMES
PRODUCTION MANAGEMENT BY CHRIS VENEZIALE

DISTRIBUTED IN NORTH AMERICA BY CHRONICLE BOOKS
85 SECOND STREET
SAN FRANCISCO, CA 94105

10 9 8 7 6 5 4 3 2

QUIRK BOOKS
215 CHURCH STREET
PHILADELPHIA, PA 19106
WWW.QUIRKBOOKS.COM

Suburban LEGENDS

TRUE TALES OF MURDER, MAYHEM, AND MINIVANS

BY SAM STALL

QUIRK BOOKS
PHILADELPHIA

CONTENTS

INTRODUCTION
IT CAME FROM SUBURBIA

Something's not quite right about the suburbs.

Even if you've never set foot in the land of cul-de-sacs, soccer moms, and neighborhood mixers, you've probably suspected as much. But if you live there or grew up there, you know it's not all pool parties and pot roast dinners. Even on the sunniest days, when the kids play in the lightly traveled streets, dads attend to their immaculately kept lawns, and moms plan their book club meetings, something still feels just a little off. Things are a bit too perfect. It's as if this great show of normalcy underscores the rampant abnormality festering just below the surface.

Well, if you feel this way about the suburbs, congratulate yourself. Because your unease is right on the money.

The hair~raising introduction, in which the author ruminates about the strangeness rampant in America's bedroom communities.

The problem with these redoubts of middle-class comfort is that the thinking behind them is fundamentally flawed. Ever since the first cornfield was platted into half-acre (.2 hectare) lots, people have flocked to such places to escape the crime, vice, and depravity of the city. But it didn't work. Because the sources of crime, vice, and depravity don't dwell in the city. They dwell in the human soul.

And no matter where we go, there they are.

I'm not saying that, when it comes to manifestations of bizarre behavior, the suburbs are any worse than other places. It's just that it seems like a bigger deal when something weird or horrible happens in a place specifically designed to keep the weird and horrible at bay. It violates the unwritten covenant of suburban living: In exchange for residing in a house only slightly more distinctive and personalized than the little red plastic ones included in Monopoly games, one is supposed to enjoy a certain insulation from life's coarser side.

That's why when someone finds, say, a headless corpse down by the docks, it's no big deal. That's where it's supposed to be. But when someone finds a headless corpse on the front lawn of a twelve-room McMansion in a place called Deer Run Vistas or Fisherman's Cove or Mountain Valley Estates, that's a story.

I've gathered together a nasty little sampler of such incidents here. This Welcome Wagon basket full of "goodies" includes a look at everything from homicidal housewives (always a favorite) to mysterious disappearances to ghosts and ghouls. This volume contains enough dark neighborhood secrets to fuel an entire season of *Desperate Housewives*, small-town sexual entanglements worthy of *Peyton Place*, and a host of supernatural doings that could have come straight from *The Twilight Zone*.

You'll never look at planned communities the same way again.

PART

INHUMANLY BAD HOUSEGUESTS

Things that go bump in the night—
and then proceed to do other deeds
far more unsettling

THE PRIME-TIME POLTERGEIST

Back in the 1950s, the Long Island suburb of Seaford, New York, looked like something straight out of *Leave It to Beaver*. The tree-shaded streets were lined with newly built middle-class housing, and the yards were packed with hoards of grade-school-aged baby boomers. That was certainly the situation at the James Hermann residence—a green and white, ranch-style home where James, his wife, Lucille, and their two children, also named James and Lucille, resided.

Most ghosts are famously camera shy. But one specter nicknamed "Popper" seemed to love showing off for the media.

But all that normalcy went out the window on February 3, 1958.

It happened in the afternoon, shortly after Lucille, thirteen, and James, twelve, came home from school. Mom, in perfect keeping with the era, was there to meet them. But this scene of suburban bliss was quickly blown away when, suddenly, several bottles in widely separate locations around the house popped their caps and spewed liquid all

Lucille Hermann battled a poltergeist that had a bottle fetish.

over the place. Everything from a jug of bleach in the basement to a container of holy water in the master bedroom emptied out in rapid succession.

Needless to say, neither Lucille, James, nor their mother was anywhere near the containers when this happened. By the time Dad got home on the train that evening, however, they'd managed to put the incident pretty much behind them. Everyone seemed ready to chalk it up as "just one of those things."

But that plan was shot out of the water two days later when, at about the same time in the afternoon as the first incident, another messy round of bottle blasts took place. On this occasion the lineup included a container of nail polish, a jug of starch, and yet more holy water. Then on Friday, the same thing happened again.

James Sr., who watched the proceedings carefully, soon developed a theory. His son was something of a science wiz. It occurred to him that the boy might be rigging the containers, perhaps with a CO_2 charge, so that they popped more or less simultaneously. But his idea lost its fizz when he confronted his son, who at the time was brushing his teeth in the bathroom, about his suspicions. In the midst of their argument, a bottle of shampoo slid across the sink under its own power and flopped to the floor.

That was enough for the old man. He called the cops, who—after grilling him for a couple of minutes to make sure he wasn't a crank—sent out a patrolman to look things over. The cop, James Hughes, found the whole thing fairly amusing, until he watched several bottles in the bathroom pop their lids and spray their contents in his direction. This got the case bumped up the chain of command to detective Joseph Tozzi, who started prowling the Hermann residence on February 11. He learned that whatever was messing with the bottles seemed to have a particular problem with the container of holy water in the bedroom, which was opened and emptied several times. On one occasion when James Sr. himself heard the cap pop, he rushed into the room and found the container on the floor. When he picked it up, it seemed unnaturally warm.

On February 15, things escalated. The kids were watching TV with a cousin when a porcelain statue rose up off a coffee table and then fell to the floor. The family decided they needed help from a more powerful force than the local constabulary, so they called in a Catholic priest to bless the house. Unfortunately this didn't stop the entity—now, for obvious reasons, nicknamed Popper—from continuing its antics.

While the inside of the abode morphed into a house of horrors, a media circus pitched its tents on the family's front lawn. Word about the ghostly infestation had gotten out, and reporters laid siege to the Hermanns. Cranks also started arriving by the busload, including a legion of "holy men" from various faiths, many of whom conducted unsolicited prayer services and exorcisms on the front lawn. Soon the story was splashed across every local paper and broadcast on TV and radio.

The public wanted to hear all the details, and Popper seemed ready and willing to oblige with new, ever-more-brash stunts. The entity allegedly threw another porcelain figure twelve feet (3.6 m), smashing it into a desk with such force that it left a dent—a dent that was duly filmed and broadcast by local television crews.

Soon objects were flying all over the house. On February 24, Detective

Tozzi found that a heavy bookcase in James Jr.'s room had toppled over. In the following days, the same impromptu moving service tipped over an encyclopedia-filled bookshelf, tossed a statue of the Virgin Mary across the master bedroom, and threw a pack of flashbulbs owned by a photographer from the *London Evening News* against the dining room wall. Clearly things were starting to escalate, and there was no logical explanation, or religious doctrine, to improve the situation.

Help arrived from the Parapsychology Laboratory at Duke University. The group was toying with the then-novel concept that poltergeist infestations are unknowingly caused by the subconscious mind. Specifically, they seemed strongly associated with teenagers in the throes of puberty. The Hermann family, with thirteen-year-old Lucille and twelve-year-old James Jr., certainly had raging hormones aplenty. Even more tellingly, the police reported that around 75 percent of the poltergeist manifestations happened in the presence of James Jr. In many of those cases (even though he was cleared of any hoaxing), he was the only witness.

The Duke program's Dr. J. Gaither Pratt paid the family a visit and spent a great deal of time talking to James Jr. During this interlude not one single Popper incident took place. However, after extensive research, and in spite of the fact that it seems extremely suspicious that when the boy was otherwise occupied, nothing "ghostly" happened, the Duke team concluded that the case wasn't a fraud.

Popper, for reasons unknown, put in his last appearance on March 10. The being went out with a comparative whimper. That evening the family was getting ready for bed when Pratt and another Duke researcher heard a loud pop from the basement. Hurrying downstairs with the family, they found an unlidded bleach bottle. And that, after sixty-seven recorded disturbances over the span of a month, was that.

Everyone from building inspectors to priests to parapsychologists visited the house during the infestation, and none could offer an explanation for the goings-on. To this day, no one can. Perhaps Lucille Hermann's original opinion of the oddities was closest to the truth. It was "just one of those things."

THE LITTLE GIRL IN THE WINDOW

A ghost in the attic becomes front-page news.

When *Indianapolis Star* photographer Mike Fender left his office on the bright, sunny morning of April 29, 1997, he had no idea he was about to take the most disturbing picture of his career. All he wanted to do was grab a few shots of a nineteenth-century Gothic Revival farmhouse that was being moved from one location to another.

It was a sight worth recording. The twenty-four-room house had perched atop a lonely hill for more than a century, until suburban development put it in jeopardy. So the Historic Landmarks Foundation of Indiana purchased the place and undertook the laborious task of moving it to a new neighborhood just down the road. Fender was there to document the process. He snapped image after image as the massive structure, carefully positioned on a heavy trailer, crawled slowly to its new resting place.

At one point he stood directly in front of the house and shot a quick series of images that took in the entire facade. In the highest window he thought he saw something odd, but it was so strange—so impossible—

that he quickly pushed it out of his mind. "I remember looking up at that window, and it looked like there was a little girl there," he recalls. "But I pretty much dismissed it because I knew that couldn't be. I just thought it was light or curtains or something like that."

But he couldn't dismiss it the next day, after the photo saw print in the *Star*. Almost immediately readers started calling, asking about the ethereal image of a girl in a blue dress. She seemed to rest her hands on the sill of the home's uppermost window as she looked down at the workmen below.

Of course, there couldn't have been a child up there. The house had been cleared before the move began. So if it wasn't a living girl, could

A newspaper photo revealed this candid shot of a "spirited" youngster (center window).

it be a ghost? That was the conclusion many readers leaped to the moment they saw the picture. "We got hundreds of calls," Fender says. "Things like this usually fade after a day or two, but this went on and on and on."

Rumors quickly circulated that the big, old house was haunted. The being in the photo was said to be the spirit of a child who had accidentally been killed by hunters while she played in the nearby woods. Others said she'd fallen from one of the home's second-story balconies and broken her neck. Another favorite asserted that she was an undead visitor from a family cemetery near the house's old hilltop location. Never mind that the Historic Landmarks Foundation of Indiana, which researched the place as part of its preservation work, found no evidence of any such events. Or that the home's new owner, Amy Cook, has so far been untroubled by spirits, in blue dresses or otherwise.

But perhaps there's another explanation. Some say that ghosts associated with a particular locale can be "awakened" if their physical surroundings are disturbed. If that's the case, then it's hard to imagine anything more profoundly disturbing than having the house you "live" in suddenly picked up, loaded onto a truck, and carted to a new location. Maybe, if it really was a girl's ghost looking out that window, she didn't plan to stay. Maybe she just wanted to witness the spectacle before going back to wherever she came from.

As for Fender, he still thinks about the picture occasionally. Back in 1997, he enlarged the image on a computer monitor so he could study the outlines of the "girl." He chalks it up to a trick of light playing on the window's screen. And of course, there's the fact that the interior of the room behind the apparition is blue, which would explain her apparel. The problem is, no matter how big one makes the picture, there's never a moment when the illusion falls apart. It still looks like a little girl—a little girl in a blue dress who has no face. No face at all.

"I'm 90 percent sure it was just some sort of optical trick," Fender says. "But I can't say that with 100 percent certainty, because you just never know."

DISTURBING DEVELOPMENTS

In September 1969, California resident Rita Swift captured some of the most mysterious images ever committed to film. But it took almost three decades for her to realize what she had seen. At the time, she lived in the suburban Orange County town of Placentia, just south of Los Angeles. An amateur photographer, she was shooting backyard pictures of everything from the family cat to a new swing set to portraits of her five-year-old daughter, Lisa. Her camera of choice that day was an antique Kodak Brownie Hawkeye, which she'd hand-loaded with black-and-white film.

Some pictures are worth a thousand words—words such as "terrifying" and "inexplicable."

Swift took the pictures, set the roll aside, and forgot about it. Nearly thirty years later, in July 1997, she stumbled across the undeveloped film in an old cedar chest. It was labeled "taken in our backyard Sept. 1969." Intrigued, she took it to a photo shop in nearby Yorba Linda to see if any of the exposures could be salvaged.

She got more—much more—than she bargained for.

The roll produced nineteen prints, the first sixteen of which contained conventional backyard scenes. But photos seventeen through nineteen were anything but conventional. The first image, for some reason, showed what appeared to be three Native Americans dancing in a row, all dressed in traditional costumes. The next two were even creepier. They revealed what looked like a large group of Native Americans in ceremonial dress, gathered around a row of bodies that were seemingly being prepared for cremation.

Obviously, nothing of the sort took place in Swift's backyard back in September 1969. But that doesn't mean it never happened. Swift has come to believe that perhaps her property hosted just such a ritual a very long time ago, and that her camera recorded its psychic residue. "I tried several times to show these photos to Native Americans, but they are afraid of them," she has said of the shots. "This is because they agree the photos are of a ritual of cremation."

Incredibly, there's a bit of hard evidence to back up her belief. In 1962, while planting a tree in the yard, the Swifts unearthed the partly cremated bones of a Native American female. The remains, according to experts at California State College in Long Beach, were roughly seven thousand years old. A few years later, the family built a living room extension over the spot where the body was found. Now the cremation site rests indoors, more or less under the family piano.

Which might explain why Swift's daughter, back when she took piano lessons, would sometimes complain about an ethereal flute that seemed to accompany her when she practiced.

There are other signs of a haunting, including strange, fast-moving black shapes that are occasionally glimpsed indoors. Even more telling, the odor of burning wood sometimes permeates the house. "Often we smell a sweet burning wood that follows us from room to room and then disappears as quickly as it comes," Swift has said.

Perhaps both the photos and the smells serve the same purpose—to give notice to the land's present tenants that its former owners are keeping an eye on things.

GUESS WHAT'S COMING TO DINNER?

These days, insidious forces ranging from video games to incessant cell phone calls conspire to keep families from sitting down in the evening and enjoying a quiet meal together. But those distractions pale in comparison to the hassles endured by the Edgar Jones family of Baltimore, Ohio, just east of Columbus.

The entity that plagued the Jones family just didn't know how to mind its manners.

The clan's troubles began on January 14, 1960, as they all sat down to dinner. Before anyone could so much as lift a fork, a decorative pottery pitcher sitting on a long display shelf near the table inexplicably exploded, pelting the surprised family with splinters and shards. Jones's wife leapt to her feet, shocked but heartsick. The piece had been part of her prized ceramics collection. Disconsolate (and more than a little puzzled), she started for the kitchen to get a broom.

Little did she know that some unseen force had decided to put her out of the crockery collecting business for good. Before she could leave the room, the other pitchers on the shelf exploded one by one, as if they were targets in a shooting gallery. Within seconds, all fifteen were reduced to piles of rubble.

But this was just the opening shot in a frantic haunting that was as intense as it was short-lived. The strange visitations would peter out on February 8, but not before the family's nerves were shot and a lot more dishes met their maker. Once, the Jones clan watched in horror as a ceramic flower pot lofted itself off a shelf and bowled through a glass window. Meals became a particular trial. During one sit-down, a sugar bowl wafted up to the ceiling, turned over, and emptied itself on the family. And on another evening, as Mrs. Jones and her daughter gamely tried to fix something to eat, a case of soda pop bottles blew their tops, hosing down the kitchen. For good measure, a row of glasses then marched off a shelf and shattered on the floor.

Soon, taking any sort of sustenance became problematic. Whenever the Joneses got together in the dining room, the light above the table would swing back and forth as if an earthquake had struck. It got so unnerving that eventually the family started eating elsewhere in the house. When they could get a moment's peace, that is. Often, in the midst of breakfast, lunch, or dinner, the utensils beside their plates would simply vanish, never to be seen again.

Fortunately, the powerful being seemed only to have it in for ceramics and glassware; it didn't seem bent on physical violence. That sort of thing happened just once. When Mrs. Jones stooped to pick up a can of corn that had been knocked off a shelf, she was promptly brained with a can of sauerkraut.

Though the entity seemed to particularly enjoy disrupting dinnertime, it didn't neglect its ghostly duties around the rest of the house. It knocked pictures off the walls, moved chairs, and caused a small table on a stairway landing to dance back and forth before hurling it down the steps. At a loss as to what to do, the family called the police. This accomplished little, other than freaking out the poor gumshoes who had to walk around the house watching the inexplicable events.

The local crime lab was enlisted to look for signs of fraud, but found nothing. Everyone from plumbers to city workers to a radio repairman were called in to offer their two cents, but none could provide a "logical" explanation, let alone the vaguest idea of what to do about the problem. Even worse, the story got out to the papers. Soon reporters literally camped on the front lawn, rubbing elbows with various purported psychics and mediums, all of them jumping at a chance to investigate the case.

Fortunately for the family's sanity, soon there was no case left to investigate. On February 8, the strangeness simply ceased. What could have been the cause? No one will ever know. But it was enough for the family that they could eat once again—and enjoy their ceramic knickknacks—in peace.

WINDBREAKER OF THE DAMNED

The world of the weird and unexplained is filled with tales of cursed or possessed objects—inanimate purveyors of woe that bring misfortune to anyone who owns them. Evil auras can reside in literally anything, from jewelry to automobiles to pieces of furniture. But for Illinois resident Salvatore D'Andrea, terror came dressed in a windbreaker.

Horror can dwell anywhere, including inside a water-resistant men's coat.

A red one, to be exact. Mr. D'Andrea's fateful encounter with this otherworldly outerwear took place in September 2004, just after he married his new wife, Jennifer, and purchased a home in the Chicago suburb of Orland Park. The place was empty when the couple moved in, save for a weird, sinister windbreaker discovered lurking in an otherwise bare closet.

Not that D'Andrea initially thought it to be all that weird and sinister. Who would? But his opinion began to change the next day, when he heard strange noises emanating from the closet.

Noises that sounded like someone crying.

That was only the beginning. Soon the home's thermostat started resetting itself, driving the temperature up and down, even though untouched by human hands. And perhaps most telling of all, in the closet that still served as the windbreaker's lair, the newlyweds' clothes rearranged themselves to suit the weather-resistant jacket's bidding. Everything red mysteriously moved to the front, while articles of other colors receded to the rear.

At least D'Andrea didn't have to spend a great deal of time wondering why he'd been so afflicted. The construction worker claims that one night, shortly after the manifestations began, he was confronted by a ghost that called itself Phil. Phil stated that he had been a friend of the home's previous owners, and that he had died while wearing the red windbreaker. He also intimated, in a sinister foreshadowing of the messy and unhygienic events to come, that he disliked pets and children.

The final straw came when the couple purchased an aquarium, only to have the water suddenly turn yellow. Shortly after the incident, Phil appeared once more and reiterated that he didn't like pets—a dislike he'd elected to underscore by urinating in the fish tank.

The D'Andreas were at their wits' end. Finally, in an effort to free their home of the restless spirit, they turned not to a psychic or an exorcist, but to eBay. The offending garment was put up for sale via the online auction service under the heading "Haunted Jacket Ghost's Name Is Phil."

The windbreaker went to a woman in Morton, Pennsylvania, for $31.50. D'Andrea put his earnings toward a new, and hopefully ghost-free, jacket. By the way, its new owner reports no problems with the paranormal. Perhaps Phil was lost in shipping.

SURREAL ESTATE

A house-buying couple discovers that their new abode comes with a spirited past—and presence.

Long before the word "suburb" was widely used, the disenchanted escaped the fuss and bother of New York City by settling in upstate towns such as Nyack. This picturesque burg sits on the west bank of the Hudson River only about twenty miles (32 km) north of Gotham but a world away in attitude and pace. In 1990, that's what drew bond trader Jeffrey Stambovsky and his wife, Patrice, to the area—and to a large Victorian-style home they found for sale there. Sure, it looked a little spooky, but what of it? They quickly forked over a $32,500 down payment for the $650,000 abode.

But as so often happens with real estate deals gone bad, unsavory information came to light after the money changed hands. This time the showstopper was something far more unusual than a leaky basement or faulty furnace. The Stambovskys first got wind of it when someone offhandedly mentioned that he'd heard they were buying "the haunted house."

Though its human owners cleared out, the ghostly denizens of this
upstate New York home elected to stay.

This came as quite a surprise to the couple, who until that moment hadn't known they were doing anything of the sort. But as they learned when they dug deeper, the place they'd committed to purchasing was allegedly a veritable halfway house for the hereafter. The seller, Helen Ackley, had for years claimed that her place contained more spirits than a package liquor store. Her accounts of ghostly manifestations had been written up in numerous publications, including *Reader's Digest*. The mansion even became a featured attraction on a haunted house walking tour of Nyack.

Over the years, Ackley, in print and in person, freely told anyone who cared to listen that her place was absolutely overrun with eighteenth- and nineteenth-century ghosts that did everything from clomping loudly up and down the stairs to opening doors and windows to switching lights on and off. Yet, strangely (or, maybe, not so strangely), when it came time to sell, no one breathed a word about this to the Stambovskys. By the time they found out, their deposit had reportedly been banked and Ackley had left for new, presumably ghost-free digs in Orlando. "We were the victims of ectoplasmic fraud," Jeffrey Stambovsky told the local media.

The couple took legal action to get their deposit back. The matter wended its way to the New York Appellate Court, which ruled in the buyers' favor. Essentially, the court stated that the Stambovskys should have been informed that the property was "haunted," because even if the ghosts weren't really there, the perception that they might be could affect the desirability of the house. And since there was no reasonable way for a potential buyer to learn of the "problem" themselves, Ackley—who had already told pretty much everyone else on the planet—was required to inform them.

Justice Israel Rubin, who wrote the majority decision (and obviously had a very good time doing so) stated that "applying the strict rule of caveat emptor to a contract involving a house possessed by poltergeists conjures up visions of a psychic or medium routinely accompanying the structural engineers and Terminix man on an inspection of every home subject to a contract of sale. In the interest of avoiding such untenable consequences, the notion that a haunting is a condition which can and should be ascertained upon reasonable inspection of the premises is a hobgoblin, which should be exorcised from the body of legal precedent and laid quietly to rest."

Thanks to this little dustup, New York home sellers are now legally bound to disclose any on-site hauntings or poltergeist infestations, just as they would termite damage or overly high radon levels. In the end, the ghost-averse Stambovskys got their money back, and Ackley had to find another buyer with stronger nerves. Maybe she didn't think the ghosts were a problem, because they'd never been a problem for *her*. Quite the opposite, in fact. According to her *Reader's Digest* article, the spirits had actually left gifts for her family, including baby rings for Ackley's grandchildren and a silver sugar tong for her.

Given their benign nature, perhaps the current owners, if they ever sell, can list the ghosts under "amenities."

THE HAUNTING OF 2115 MARTINGALE DRIVE

One has to wonder why ghosts bother haunting the living. How could frightening children, slamming doors, and tromping invisibly up and down the basement steps hold any fascination for a soul that has divested itself of its physical form? What possible interest could worldly affairs have for such an otherworldly creature?

Some ghosts don't want to cause trouble or spread terror. They just want a little recognition.

For centuries, everyone from parapsychologists to psychics to ordinary folk have pondered these questions. But every once in a while, a particular ghost manages to make the reason for its presence known. Which means that we occasionally get the chance to right a wrong that keeps a spirit earthbound, allowing it to depart in peace.

Such was the case for Sybrand Broersma—formerly an Oklahoma University physics professor and now a resident of the Great Beyond.

Broersma was born in 1919 in the Netherlands, where he earned advanced degrees in physics before moving to the United States and becoming a citizen in 1957. He joined the Oklahoma University faculty in 1959 and became a full professor in 1986. Broersma, a lifelong bachelor, lived alone in a quiet suburban neighborhood in a house he built in 1981 at 2115 Martingale Drive.

It was there that, on or about December 20, 1987, he died of natural causes. His body wasn't discovered until December 27, when a student stopped by to check on him.

Afterward, his expansive, cream-colored home passed to a new owner. And then to another. And then, reportedly, to another. Each purchaser stayed for a bit, then suddenly found a reason to leave. Rapidly. Some evacuated the premises so quickly that they left their personal possessions behind.

The next tenants were Jon and Agi Lurtz. Jon bought the place in 1993, and Agi moved in a year later when the couple got married. Almost immediately, she sensed that they weren't alone. In the middle of the night, the Lurtzes would awake to the sound of old-time radio shows emanating from . . . somewhere. It certainly wasn't coming from any of the home's radios. Finally, after long and fruitless searches, Agi came to a sobering conclusion. "The sound was coming from between the floors," she told the *Norman Transcript*. "It was old radio news and old TV news, very loud."

That was only the beginning. The entity sharing the house with them seemed to indulge in all the usual ghostly pranks, from popping light-bulbs to tossing small objects around to making a general racket. But its real forte was music. In addition to causing old-time radio news shows to blast from the floors, the ghost also liked to jam to the German metal band Rammstein. Interestingly, these tunes came not from the woodwork, but from the family stereo. "Sometimes it would be blaring when we'd get home," Agi told the *Transcript*. "We'd shut it off, and it would come back on."

Fortunately for the ghost, Agi had lived in haunted houses before. She could be quite fearless in the being's presence—not that she ever felt there was much to fear from the light-fixture-destroying, Teutonic-

An overdue obituary was all it took to clear a spirit out of this Oklahoma house.

techno-pop-loving entity. Which was good news, considering what happened next. Late one night in 1998, Agi awoke to find an apparition standing at the foot of her bed. Assuming it was the late professor Broersma, she asked him why he hung around. To her surprise, he replied in broken English, "Because I never had an obituary."

That weekend, Agi visited the Norman Public Library and perused back issues of the *Norman Transcript*. She learned that the entity was correct. Broersma's passing hadn't rated so much as a word on the obit page. "I guess he felt like he deserved that," she told the *Transcript*. "He needed that before he could go on."

And so Agi arranged a better-late-than-never memorial service, which was duly featured in the paper—along with the long-awaited obituary. As it turns out, the ghost's irritation at being overlooked was justified. During World War II, Broersma had been a member of the Dutch resistance, barely escaping capture and execution by the Nazis. And at Oklahoma University, he helped NASA develop some of the first genuinely useful sensors for use aboard satellites.

Giving the old professor his due seems to have worked. Since his moment in the sun, Agi reports that Broersma's house is now quiet.

GHOST DAD

Every baby boomer of a certain age remembers Ozzie Nelson. The creator and star of *The Adventures of Ozzie and Harriet*, he was the prototype TV dad for the very first generation of raised-on-the-boob-tube Americans. But they might not realize just how closely the pro-

Death wasn't the final act for one of TV's most revered sitcom fathers.

gram mirrored Nelson's actual life. Or that, years after his death, he can't seem to relinquish his most famous role.

Nelson harbored an almost insatiable desire to build a screen life that was just like his private existence. His pretend spouse, the former Harriet Hilliard, was also his real wife. Likewise, his TV sons were his real offspring, David and Ricky. Ozzie's character had once been a big band leader, and his wife a singer—exactly what the real Nelsons had done before they developed a radio comedy show and then brought their shtick to TV. Even their television home was a copy of their actual Colonial-style abode, located in one of the less-ostentatious parts of Los Angeles's most famous suburb, Hollywood.

It was almost like a modern reality show, except funnier and without bitter arguments or trash talk. The Nelson clan dwelled in this strange-but-homey alternate universe for fourteen years. After the show ended, Ozzie did some producing and directing work and put together a short-lived early seventies syndicated sitcom called *Ozzie's Girls*. And then, in 1975 at the age of sixty-nine, he died of cancer and was buried in Forest Lawn Cemetery.

But as the old-time TV commercials used to say, "Wait, there's more."

It seems that when the Grim Reaper called "cut," Nelson refused to take his final bow. Those who have lived in his former residence at 1822 Camino Palmiero report that the place is absolutely filled with his ghostly presence. Nelson, who during his mortal days was famous for his work ethic, now seems to spend his time studiously pursuing such ghostlike activities as opening and closing doors, messing with bathroom faucets, and turning lights on and off. One female owner (the house has changed hands several times) even made the outlandish claim that some unseen force repeatedly felt her up while she slept.

Others say they've actually seen the ghostly figure of the famous father figure wafting from room to room. What's surprising, and more than a little unsettling, is that this former king of comedy doesn't look like he's having a very good time. Witnesses say Nelson, who in life was an upbeat, energetic kind of guy, seems in death to have become rather sad and morose.

But perhaps he has his reasons. A man who loved his family above all else has now become some sort of ectoplasmic empty nester, watching as the house he lived in for more than three decades passes from one group of strangers to the next. And to top it off, one of them actually accused the old-school authority figure of sexual misconduct.

One can only wonder how things will turn out. Will Ozzie stay at his old house or move on to a higher plane of existence? Where, exactly, are Harriet (who died in 1994) and Ricky (who died in a plane crash in 1985)? And is it really so wrong for a lonely spirit to cop a feel now and then? Not that we're saying he actually did, of course.

Stay tuned.

The Nelson family during happier times.

TERROR BY DESIGN

These days the cable channels are overrun with shows like *Trading Spaces*, which turn the onerous task of redecorating one's home into cheap entertainment. And if the person whose home is being overhauled seems less than thrilled with the final result, so much the better. Frowns and snide comments make for interesting television.

It's definitely not a good thing when a home's ghosts take exception to your decorating plans.

But that's often not how it works in the real world. Or in the surreal world, for that matter. Before you start moving the couch around or changing window treatments, it's always wise to consider how all the home's residents—both living and dead—will react. That's a bit of wisdom that Frances Freeborn of Bakersfield, California, had to learn the hard way.

Freeborn moved into her new house in November 1981, and she immediately set about changing things. She could hardly be faulted, because nothing had been touched since the recent, sudden demise of the abode's previous owner, Meg Lyons. The woman's furnishings still filled the place, and her clothes even hung in the closets. Clearly, it all had to go.

But though this was a no-brainer to Freeborn (as it probably would be to anyone else with a pulse), it didn't sit well with the home's former resident. The newly deceased Ms. Lyons initially registered her displeasure by making loud thumping noises in the kitchen—a problem Freeborn at first ascribed to noisy plumbing. But it was harder to explain why the kitchen cabinets, scrupulously closed before bedtime, were always found wide open in the morning. Or why lights that were turned off before she left the house were blazing when she returned.

Freeborn began to suspect she was dealing with more than bad plumbing and faulty wiring when an unseen force started challenging, and in some cases undoing, her decorating decisions. For instance, the morning after she hung a triptych of three pre—Civil War women, she found it off its hook and on the floor, propped against the wall. Freeborn repeatedly rehung the piece, only to have it taken down five times and deposited, undamaged, on the floor. Finally, following her instincts, she took the picture to another room and hung it there, where it stayed unmolested. She found out why when Lyons's son-in-law, Luke Cowley, paid a visit. He said that his mother-in-law had kept a similar picture in exactly that spot.

Apparently Freeborn still didn't understand the need to leave well enough alone. In 1982, she decided to redecorate the master bedroom, which set off a frenzy of ghostly manifestations. The disruption and unease was so strong that, even when she went out to buy paint and wallpaper, she felt as if someone were watching—and not approving. Late one night, at around 2:00 A.M., she had her suspicions confirmed. While she was washing her hands, the bathroom window suddenly flew open. She closed it and retreated back to the bedroom. Suddenly the bathroom window opened again—at the same time the bedroom window slammed shut. To make things even worse, one closet door opened while another thudded closed.

That was all Freeborn needed to see. She grabbed her hysterically barking dog and ran out into the hallway—straight into some sort of invisible, and decidedly unfriendly, entity. "There was a zone of pressure," she reportedly said. "A mass out in the hall, as if something ominous and ugly were concentrated there. I realized I had to get out of the house or I would die."

Freeborn screamed "Get out of my way!" and pushed past the creatures in the hall. Then she ran—and kept running all the way to her car. She piled in and sped away, still in her nightgown.

There's no word on how the rest of the redecorating went.

LIGHT MY FIRE

The German word "poltergeist" means, literally, "knocking spirit." This particularly nerve-wracking form of ghostly activity usually lives up to that title by rapping on walls, tossing crockery, and generally making itself a royal pain in the posterior. But not every polter-

Where there's smoke, there's a pyromaniac poltergeist.

geist confines itself to annoying but mostly harmless pursuits. One such manifestation, which took place in the Chicago suburb of Orland Hills, could easily have brought about disaster and death.

Because this particular entity didn't rap on walls. It played with fire.

It happened to the Gallo family, who resided on 169th Street in Orland Hills. On March 14, 1988, one of the clan's teenage daughters, Dina, heard a strange popping sound, followed by a shower of sparks from an electrical outlet that set a nearby pair of curtains ablaze. Dina managed to put out the conflagration and then called the fire department, but they could find no reason for the problem.

Everything was fine for a couple of days, until Dina noticed that the plug to the kitchen microwave was smoking. She immediately unplugged it, but a subsequent investigation found nothing wrong with the appliance.

Things were getting serious. Shortly thereafter, several family members heard a telltale popping sound and smelled smoke. Rushing to its source—an empty room—they discovered that a set of drapes had caught fire, along with a portion of the carpet. Yet somehow, for some reason, the blaze had done its damage, then gone out on its own. But there would be more. The next time, a desk and a set of curtains in an upstairs room were incinerated.

This incident required the intervention of the Orland Hills Fire Department, the members of which would become regular visitors to the Gallo residence. The curious part was that the blaze conducted itself in a very unblazelike manner. Objects that were within easy reach of the flames and should have been consumed remained untouched.

The local firefighters were understandably concerned about the rash of unexplained ignitions and desperate to get a handle on the cause before someone got hurt. Over the next few days, they returned more than a dozen times, trying to get to the root of the potentially deadly problem. Engineers examined the home's electrical system. Commonwealth Edison checked the outside lines to see if some sort of intermittent current buildup could be at fault. But they found nothing out of the ordinary.

Actually, something *was* out of the ordinary, but it seemingly had nothing to do with the local power grid. During the exhaustive testing, the juice to the entire house was switched off. But somehow, several outlets still started smoking, even though there shouldn't have been any current reaching them. This convinced the homeowners and investigators that, even if they couldn't trace the defect to its source, there were obviously some wires crossed somewhere. As a precaution, the home's entire electrical system was ripped out and replaced.

But the new wiring didn't end the problem. In fact, it got worse—not to mention scarier. Family members—and even some of the fire officials who still regularly visited the place—sometimes encountered a dense, white fog that smelled of sulfur. And to top it off, the brand-new outlets started sparking, just as the old ones had.

By now, the harassed firefighters were almost as familiar with the Gallo residence as the family itself was. They were there constantly, either trying to figure out where the sulfur smell came from or answering an unending series of distress calls. But though many of them smelled the noxious fumes and even complained of headaches from exposure to them, meters set up to monitor carbon monoxide levels and other gases failed to register anything.

April 7, 1988, was a particularly big day. Shortly after an official from the Illinois fire marshal's office inspected the place, the weird haze manifested itself. Burn marks appeared around several outlets, and a two-foot (1.8 m) long blue flame jetted out of one. A mattress was also consumed in a sudden conflagration. The damage was so severe that experts estimated the bedding must have been exposed to temperatures between 1,500 and 2,000 degrees Fahrenheit (815–1,100°C).

Stumped, the firefighters allegedly turned to a local paranormal investigator for help. After speaking to the family and to neighbors (who informed them, tellingly, that the Gallo house had always had a reputation for being haunted), they concluded that daughter Dina seemed to be the earthly vector through which the pyromaniac entity acted. All the fire incidents happened not just when she was in the house, but when she was very close to the site of the blaze.

Furthermore, the investigators intimated that three graves had been discovered on the property during the home's construction. However, this was repeatedly denied when the story of the Gallo house doings hit the local media.

Whatever the reason for the fires, the Gallos and their equally harassed insurance company finally agreed on a draconian solution. The home was demolished, and a new one was built in its place. Apparently this did the trick, because since then no new fires have broken out.

But there was also another critical occurrence at this time. Dina got older. Perhaps, as her raging teen hormones settled down, she ceased to be a good medium for the poltergeist, or whatever it was, to work through. That's the good news. The bad news is that, if another kid of the appropriate age and demeanor ever moves into the house, the outlets might start smoking again.

All the more reason to sleep lightly—and to keep 911 on speed dial.

MAKE ROOM FOR DANNY

Some ghosts like to haunt home furnishings instead of actual homes.

At first glance, Savannah, Georgia, antiques dealer Al Cobb seems like the last person in the world to unwittingly bring a ghost into his home. A longtime resident of what is (or by all rights should be) one of America's most-haunted locales, he's professed to numerous run-ins with the spirits said to infest his town's antebellum homes and businesses. He's even written a couple of local bestsellers on the topic.

But what Al didn't seem to realize—until it was too late—was that ghosts can haunt not just places, but things. And that in a town where some claim that specters literally glide down the streets at night, it's not a good idea to haul home strange antiques without first digging up their history.

The Cobb family learned this lesson the hard way, when in 1998 Al purchased an ornate nineteenth-century bed for his then-fourteen-year-old son, Jason. He knew little about the piece, other than that it was originally from Wilmington, North Carolina. But soon the entire Cobb family would know its story. The information came courtesy of the lively, occasionally combative spirit that during its mortal days slept there and, reportedly, also died there.

Almost immediately after setting up the piece, the Cobbs knew they'd acquired something more than just a bit of furniture. During his third night in the bed, Jason suddenly had an uneasy feeling. Though he saw nothing, he felt as if something was sprawled across the bed with its elbows on the corner of his pillow, watching him. He even thought he could feel its icy breath on his neck. "The next night he noticed the photo of his deceased grandparents on his wicker night-stand flipped down," reported the *Savannah Morning News*. "So he righted it. The next day, the photo was facing down again."

Later that same day, the family found a pile of toys heaped up in the middle of the mattress—toys that neither Jason nor his siblings, Lee and Jennifer, professed to have put there.

Al, figuring they had a ghost on their hands, first called out to the entity. When he got no response, he set out some paper and crayons and shooed everyone from the room. When the family returned in fifteen minutes, they reportedly found the words "Danny, 7" scrawled in child-like letters on one page.

According to Al, the Casper-like spirit followed up this initial note with a full-blown letter-writing campaign. Danny stated that his mother had died on the bed, and that he (who had expired on it himself in 1899) planned to stay nearby. Furthermore, no one else should go near it. That worked fine for Jason, who had already abandoned his room to the otherworldly houseguest. But not before, in a singular display of bad judgment, he taunted the spirit by lying down on its bed and pretending to take a nap. Shortly thereafter, Danny made his feelings about the imposition known. "I doubled back in the room to pick up my clothes," Jason told the *Morning News*, "when this terra cotta head that had been hanging on the wall came flying through the room, just missing me before it smashed on the floor."

So Danny had a temper. And like any seven-year-old, he liked to get into trouble. Besides scratching out enough notes to fill a diary, he darted around the house lighting candles, rummaging through drawers, and moving furniture. He also, if the Cobbs are to be believed, got other spirits to come and join him. One, named Jill, also started leaving notes, including one inviting the living family to what she called "a party in the living room."

Incredibly, the Cobbs took these otherworldly visitors in stride, showing far more patience and forbearance than would most families beset by out-of-town guests. Perhaps it was because Danny would obligingly relay messages back and forth between the family and their deceased relatives, including Al's father and the parents of his wife, Lila. The Cobbs' children even saw the boy materialize on occasion— once running around the family Christmas tree at fantastic speed.

It was a good thing the ghosts weren't too overbearing, because nothing the Cobbs tried would make them leave. Sprinkling holy water around the house accomplished nothing. Nor did getting rid of the bed that Danny was allegedly so fond of. A parapsychologist the family consulted asserted that there was some sort of energy gateway in the wall of Jason's room and that the psychically charged bed had somehow "activated" the portal, allowing Danny and other entities to get through.

Whatever the true case may be, the visitations lasted about two years before mostly petering out. But though Danny hasn't been heard from in quite a while, the Cobbs still report occasional household disturbances. For instance, every once in a while the dog's wicker bed somehow gets dragged to the top of the stairs. Maybe it's just a calling card from the ghosts, so that everyone realizes they aren't gone, and shouldn't be forgotten.

PART

THE GHOUL
NEXT DOOR

Terrible tales about infamous miscreants
who, according to their neighbors, were
"quiet and never made any trouble"

HISTORIC PRESERVATION

Some people keep their deceased loved ones in their hearts. Others keep them in their basement.

La Crosse, Wisconsin, is one of those bucolic Midwestern summer resort communities that uses its beautiful scenery, quaint but trendy shops, and gorgeous lakes to attract out-of-town-ers during the warm months. Straddling the banks of the Mississippi River about an hour downstream from Minneapolis/St. Paul, its sylvan setting reminds one of the Old Country. The tourist bureau even offers brochures in German and Norwegian.

But lately the area has become known for something else—something that will definitely not be mentioned in the travel flyers.

This sunny slice of Scandinavian-style heaven was also home to a man who kept a corpse in his basement. But unlike other people involved in such scenarios, he wasn't a monster. He wasn't even that bad of a person. He was just caught up in a really weird situation—one that he coped with in a spectacularly weird way.

His name was Philip Schuth, and he spent almost all of his fifty-two years in a small house on French Island, a tiny community on the fringe of La Crosse. Schuth was, to put it mildly, not a regular guy. But that's to be expected, considering that his upbringing wasn't exactly regular either. The full story would provide enough fodder for two Lifetime movies—if Lifetime did movies about weird, socially stunted men. But the highlights are appalling enough.

His mother, Margie, was an English war bride brought home to Wisconsin by Philip's "father," James Schuth. James wasn't exactly a knight in shining armor. A loud, abusive jerk, he exploited the fact that his wife was stranded thousands of miles from her family. He told Margie, who never held a job or even learned how to drive, that if she divorced him she would starve on the streets, along with her "little bastard." This, reportedly, was Dad's pet name for the boy, whom he regularly beat and sexually abused. It wasn't until years later, when Schuth learned James wasn't his biological father, that he realized the full meaning of the remark.

Not that Mom was much of a help. Convinced she was a stranger in a strange land, she clung to her son for support. She walked Schuth to class every day, from grade school right through high school. As one

Emergency crews give Mom a ride to the mortuary.

can imagine, this sort of thing didn't exactly endear him to his class-mates. Nor did the fact that he'd acquired an absurdly out-of-place English accent from spending all his time with his dear mum.

But in spite of all this, he somehow became a National Honor Society member who went on to graduate from the University of Wisconsin—La Crosse with honors. Unfortunately, his chosen field, teaching, couldn't have been a worse fit. His lack of rapport with the kids (or with anyone else, for that matter) led one of his advisors to tell him that he simply wasn't cut out for the profession.

Philip Schuth earned the nickname "Frosty" in jail.

As it turned out, this book-smart man didn't seem cut out for much of anything. Extremely shy, socially inept, and almost nonverbal around strangers, he earned a meager living washing dishes at a restaurant, working as a security guard at a hardware store, and doing other menial tasks. At least his "father," who died in 1994, was no longer around. That left just him and an increasingly frail and elderly Margie, both living in the same house they'd occupied for decades.

At this point one could almost understand if Schuth, who had been through years of what amounted to Serial Killer Training School, had started whacking strangers and burying them in his basement. But what he did instead—the thing that would one day draw him into a showdown with a SWAT team—was in some ways even more disturbing.

On August 15, 2000, the mama's boy lost his mama. Schuth discovered that Margie, eighty-six, had passed away from heart and kidney failure (as later determined by coroners).

Of course, the normal thing to do would have been to call the authorities. But Schuth didn't seem interested in—or, perhaps, wasn't capable of—doing the normal thing. According to conversations he had with the *La Crosse Tribune*, he feared the police would accuse him of killing her.

So he decided not to tell anyone.

Instead, he took his mother's body to the basement, gently folded it into a sitting position, and deposited it in a trunk freezer. There she would remain, unknown to the world, for four and a half years.

With Mom gone, Schuth got down to the serious business of becoming a recluse. Making only rare excursions to the grocery store (and living off Margie's Social Security checks, which kept arriving like clockwork), he let the house fall to ruin around him. The roof leaked severely, and most of the utilities either fritzed out or were shut off. Eventually Schuth was reduced to gathering drinking water by dragging plastic drums out into the yard to catch the rain.

But through it all, he kept the freezer cold and the cable TV service connected.

Nosy visitors weren't a problem, because Schuth had absolutely no friends. Anyone who happened to inquire about his mother was simply told she was sick or otherwise indisposed. Incredibly, not even the state of his property roused any interest from authorities. Nor did the fact that he became the target of choice for neighborhood vandals, who did everything from shooting at him with BB guns to physically assaulting him in his own front yard.

It was one such act that finally put a spotlight on Schuth's peculiar living arrangement. On April 22, 2004, he allegedly caught a couple of neighborhood kids vandalizing his steps. Schuth reportedly came out of the house and, in the process of running them off, smacked ten-year-old Josh Russell in the face. The boy ran home and told his parents, who quickly confronted their neighbor. But Schuth, rather than talk it over, pulled out a pistol and started shooting. He clipped the boy's dad three times, but none of the injuries were serious.

This outburst brought out the local SWAT team, which surrounded the house. After a standoff that dragged on through the night, Schuth surrendered. Once inside, police found homemade bombs, a cache of firearms—and, of course, Margie.

Schuth (after psychiatrists declared him mentally competent) was charged with a slew of crimes, among them attempted first-degree homicide, hiding a corpse, and a grab bag of weapons-related offenses. Sadly, for a man who spent most of his childhood being tormented by strangers, life in jail turned out to be more of the same. The other inmates took to calling him "Frosty," among other things, and suggested he sell his infamous freezer on eBay.

Worst of all, local entrepreneurs climbed on the bandwagon. A T-shirt vendor made clothing commemorating Schuth's crimes. And, in the final insult, someone started selling magnets that say "My Mom Is Cooler Than Yours."

They are, of course, refrigerator magnets.

FAMILY GUY

Sometimes, keeping up appearances can be murder.

John List, forty-six, was a strait-laced, buttoned-down Lutheran who could have made Ward Cleaver look like Homer Simpson. God-fearing, taciturn, and (by all accounts) wound as tight as a cheap watch, the part-time Sunday school teacher lived for years in a nineteen-room, three-story Victorian mansion in one of the nicest upper-middle-class neighborhoods in Westfield, New Jersey. He seemed devoted to his wife, Helen, his daughter, Patty, his two sons, John Jr. and Frederick, and his eighty-five-year-old mother, who lived in an apartment on the home's top floor.

Which was why everyone was so surprised when he murdered the lot of them and disappeared.

The problem (though no one understood its severity until it was too late) was that List was a control freak. An accountant, he'd risen steadily at the New Jersey firm where he worked, eventually becoming a vice president. At home, the man was so fastidious that he mowed his lawn in a suit and tie. When it came to his personal life, he wanted everything—and everyone—in its place.

The List residence, before a fire destroyed it.

Not surprisingly, it didn't work out that way. And it slowly drove him nuts.

Take the beautiful house. When List moved to Westfield from Michigan in the sixties, he'd used the proceeds from the sale of his mother's home to help purchase his new, sprawling abode, which was so palatial it included a ballroom with a leaded glass ceiling. Unfortunately, the family never had the cash to fully furnish the place. For the entire time the Lists lived there, their voices echoed through largely empty rooms.

The family was hardly a model of domestic bliss. List and his mother were deeply into religion—an interest the rest of the family didn't share. Particularly his daughter, Patty. She was active in local theater and (at least to her father) something of a wild child. The sixteen-year-old was rumored to have dabbled in witchcraft, and she had a couple of minor run-ins with the cops for being out late and smoking. Even worse, List's wife was slowly dying from a dose of syphilis contracted from her first husband, who was killed in World War II. By the early seventies, Helen List was nearly blind and losing her grip on reality.

Things finally, irrevocably spun out of control when List lost his accounting job. Incredibly, he kept the news from his family, leaving the house each day at his usual time, going to the Westfield train station, and then hanging around until "quitting time" arrived and he could go home.

In October 1971, he applied for a gun permit. He said he wanted it for home protection, but he had something far more lethal in mind.

List's was the most premeditated of murder sprees. On November 9, he had milk and mail deliveries stopped and told the schools his kids

John List, far left, with his soon-to-be-deceased wife and kids.

attended that they were going on an emergency trip to visit his wife's sick mother in North Carolina.

Two days later, List set his plan in motion. After the kids went to school, he sat down with his wife at the breakfast table and shot her in the head. Then he went upstairs to his mother's apartment and gave her the same treatment. Next he placed Helen's body on top of a sleeping bag and dragged it into the home's magnificent ballroom. Then, incredibly, he returned to the table and finished eating breakfast. He'd need his strength for what came next.

That afternoon he picked up Patty at school, drove her home, shot her before she could even take her coat off, put her on a sleeping bag, and dragged her into the ballroom. Then he picked up his younger son, Frederick, at school and repeated the process. Finally, when his older son, John Jr., came home, he shot him and deposited the body, with all the rest, in the ballroom.

With the corpses of his loved ones neatly arranged, he calmly ate dinner and went to bed. The next morning he disappeared.

He enjoyed an excellent head start. Everyone, it seemed, fell for the "going on a trip" ploy. It wasn't until December 7 that a neighbor, unsettled by the home's appearance, finally called police. All the lights inside had been blazing twenty-four hours a day, and now some of them were burning out. During that same time, Patty's drama coach, Ed Illiano, made several fruitless trips to the house. Patty, it seemed, was supposed to be rehearsing for a play, and her absence without so much as a note of explanation was troubling. He arrived at the List residence for another visit at roughly the same time the police did.

When the cops finally forced their way in, they found the heat off and the interior freezing cold. Eerily, loud church music played over the home's intercom system. They followed dried blood trails down the hallways to the ballroom, where they saw four bodies—bodies that Illiano immediately identified as those of the List family. Everyone was there except for Dad. Having murdered his family, John List wrote a three-page note of explanation to his minister, then headed for the hills. He wouldn't turn up again until 1989.

After the killings, he'd taken trains to Michigan and then Denver. Once in Colorado, he took the name Robert Clark. Ever the Bible-thumper, he eventually married a woman he met at his local church. An anonymous tip to the FBI finally undid him. He was living in Virginia when his case was profiled on the TV show *America's Most Wanted*. Ironically, List was a big fan of the program but happened to miss that particular episode. If he'd seen it, he might have blown town before the law caught up with him. But that wasn't how it turned out. List was extradited to New Jersey, tried, and convicted. These days the only prayer groups he attends are the ones at Trenton State Prison.

Some have theorized that List felt the only way to save his family from humiliation and destitution was to kill them. However, if that's the case, why didn't he elect to join them in death?

And even more to the point, why didn't he bother to take advantage of the source of ready cash that was, literally, right above his head? It seems that the ceiling in the ballroom—the same ballroom where List laid out the slaughtered remains of his family—was decorated with a signed Tiffany glass ceiling. If he'd sold it, the cash would probably have paid the mortgage on his house, with plenty left over.

Instead, it was lost years later when the List house burned down under mysterious circumstances.

DEMOLITION MAN

A wise old sage (Arnold Schwarzenegger, perhaps?) once said, "Don't get mad, get even." But disgruntled businessman Marvin Heemeyer did both. First, he got extremely mad at the residents of the Colorado resort town of Granby for slights both real and (mostly) imagined. Then he got even.

Never antagonize someone who has a short fuse, a long memory, and a big bulldozer.

Perhaps a little more than even. After months of single-minded work and planning, on June 4, 2004, he unleashed a revenge so diabolical, so destructive, and so bizarre, that it was worthy of a James Bond villain.

They'll certainly never forget about it in Granby—the parts that are still standing, that is.

Like most stories of crazed retribution, this reckoning was a long time in coming. Heemeyer moved to Colorado from South Dakota, and by the early nineties he'd built up a chain of successful muffler shops in nearby Boulder. The money was good enough to allow him to move to the resort community of Grand Lake, about sixteen miles from

Granby. In 1992, he opened up a Granby operation called Mountain View Muffler.

When he wasn't riding a snowmobile, hiking, or otherwise enjoying the great outdoors, Heemeyer dabbled in various civic causes. Trouble was, he often didn't get his way—and he was a sore loser. In 1994, he championed a failed attempt to bring gambling to Grand Lake. He didn't take kindly to the proposal's defeat, and during the struggle he almost came to blows with the town's newspaper editor, who opposed the measure.

Things got even uglier in 2000, when the town of Granby started a debate over whether to locate a concrete plant next to Heemeyer's muffler shop. He said he was angered by the noise and dust the project might create. But he also had a problem with the project's operator, Cody Docheff, to whom he'd made an abortive attempt to sell his property. The Granby town board tried to referee the sparring match between the two, but it was obvious to those involved that it was metastasizing into something far more personal and venomous than just a hassle over a bit of territory.

Marvin Heemeyer's bullet-proof, sixty-one ton bulldozer.

In 2001, the town board finally decided in favor of the plant. Heemeyer filed a lawsuit challenging the decision, which also failed. Then, in 2003, he got into another dustup with the city over whether his muffler shop had to be hooked up to the city sewer system. It seemed like small potatoes, and to a person with adequate anger-management skills, it *would* have been small potatoes. But in Heemeyer's mind it became a very, very big problem.

Unknown to anyone at the time, he started plotting his revenge—the instrument of which would be a sixty-one-ton (55 metric ton) bull-dozer he'd purchased several years earlier and stored in a building next to Mountain View Muffler. In December 2003, he sold both the shop and the building housing the dozer, with the proviso that he keep the use of the two-thousand-square-foot (185 sq m), walled-off section where the massive machine sat. In March of that same year, he also deeded his house to a friend, then moved into the work space to do some serious customizing.

Heemeyer's death dozer tossed a pickup truck through the offices of a construction firm.

It was quite a job for one man—even a man fueled by a highly unstable mix of rage and lust for vengeance. Heemeyer, an expert welder, slowly turned his civilian bulldozer into an armored war machine. First he shielded the cab by sheathing it in two layers of heavy steel with concrete poured between them. He could keep tabs on the outside world by looking at three TV monitors linked to exterior cameras encased in shatterproof, high-impact plastic. Three high-powered rifles were mounted inside this fortified redoubt, pointing fore, aft, and to one side.

The neighbors got their first look at Heemeyer's pimped-out ride on the fateful afternoon of June 4. According to some reports, before he climbed into the bulldozer's armored cab and bolted the hatch shut behind him, he greased the exterior to prevent attackers from scrambling up its sides. Of course there wasn't a door in the building big enough for the dozer to drive through, but that wasn't a problem. Heemeyer simply fired up the machine's 410-horsepower (305 kw) engine, pointed it at the nearest wall, and made one.

The first target, not surprisingly, was the cement plant next door. Heemeyer's machine pulverized the company's administrative building with the ease of a smoker grinding out a cigarette butt. Then he took off the back half of the factory proper. All this in spite of the fact that Docheff, Heemeyer's nemesis, quickly climbed aboard his own piece of heavy construction equipment and tried in vain to stop the destruction by ramming the armored bulldozer.

Once he was satisfied with the level of carnage, Heemeyer went calling on folks in town. Rumbling down Granby's main drag with an ever-growing line of police vehicles in pursuit, he took the front off the headquarters of the local electric company, tossed a pickup truck into the offices of a construction firm, annihilated the town hall, and smashed the office and printing plant of the local newspaper, the *Sky-Hi News*. Police peppered the massive rig with bullets, but their small arms were useless against the moving metal mountain. "I watched a police officer fire many rounds at it, and he may as well have been using a squirt gun," one bystander told CBS News.

Then Heemeyer, who had written a list of targets that he carried along with him on his rampage, ran over the home of the town's deceased ex-mayor. Next it was on to the Independent Gas Company, where he spent a few minutes trying to ignite the company's propane storage tanks by firing at them with a .50-caliber rifle. Failing at that, he then trundled up to a hardware store (owned by a town board member) and leveled it. But during the process, the engine finally gave out on his dozer. Police quickly swarmed the vehicle, and moments later a single gunshot from inside was heard. Heemeyer had killed himself with a pistol. In a final, macabre salute to his workmanship, it took hours to extract his body from the cab.

In retrospect, his choice of vengeance was as unique as it was inexplicable. One of the biggest mysteries isn't how he managed to keep such an elaborate plan secret, but why he bothered with something so ridiculously excessive in the first place. The bottom line is that a zoning dispute and some sewer work cost him his life. Perhaps, considering the final outcome, the better approach would have been to shrug the whole thing off.

He may have left an indelible imprint on the memories of Granby's inhabitants, but not on their real estate. Insurance money quickly replaced what was damaged. Even the concrete plant, the focus of so much ire, was back in operation almost immediately. Still, there was one lasting civic improvement: Sour grapes Heemeyer and his killer bulldozer were no more.

THE RANDY RABBI

Rabbi Fred J. Neulander was a speaker of polished eloquence. Many times he'd used that gift to enthrall the members of his synagogue, Congregation M'Kor Shalom. Situated in the upscale town of Cherry Hill, New Jersey, a suburb of Philadelphia, it was one of the state's largest reform congregations. Neulander and his wife, Carol, had cofounded it.

This holy man's way of settling his marriage problems wasn't exactly kosher.

But the sixty-one-year-old rabbi never needed his golden voice more desperately than on a Friday in 2002. It wasn't so that he could enliven a bar mitzvah or offer a memorable comment at a wedding. He needed it to save his life. Because on this occasion, he addressed not an audience of adoring followers, but a courtroom packed with onlookers out for his blood (including two of his three children), and a jury that had just found him guilty of murder and was now pondering whether to send him to death row.

Neulander had been convicted, after a four-week trial, of capital murder, felony murder, and conspiracy—specifically, of having two goons bludgeon his wife to death on November 1, 1994. That was the worst, but not the only, part of the horrendous tale. During the lengthy investigation and the court proceedings that followed, it was also revealed that this former pillar of his community was a serial womanizer who'd had repeated affairs with female congregants—including with a woman named Victoria Lombardi, perhaps better known as Miss Vicki, Tiny Tim's ex-wife.

But it was another liaison, with a former Philadelphia-area radio-talk-show host, that allegedly prompted the rabbi to have his wife savagely murdered in the living room of their home.

It was a sordid end to what had looked like a very successful marriage. Neulander had grown up in Queens, New York. After college, he became a rabbi (the sixth generation of his family to do so) and married, over her parents' objections, Carol Toby Lidz, who hailed from a well-to-do Woodmere, New York, family. In the early seventies they moved to Cherry Hill to raise their three kids. In 1974, they founded M'Kor Shalom.

Carol became the successful owner of a baking business, and Neulander was respected, even revered. But mere adulation wasn't enough. The rabbi also craved love and approval of a more crass, physical sort. So he started fooling around with members of his congregation.

His most precious conquest was Elaine Soncini, a former Philadelphia radio personality who turned to Neulander for grief counseling after her husband died of cancer in late 1992. But soon their relationship developed into a torrid two-year affair—one that indirectly led to Carol Neulander's death. The couple allegedly met for sex as often as seven times a week, occasionally in the rabbi's office at M'Kor Shalom. Finally, Soncini got tired of playing the other woman and pressured Neulander to leave his wife.

The rabbi told her that if he did, he'd probably lose his job. But he also intimated that they would be together soon. He predicted his wife and the mother of his children was due for a "tumultuous fall," and that "violence was coming to Carol."

He certainly should have known. Because he was the one bringing it.

Unbeknownst to anyone, Neulander was laying the groundwork for murder. In 1993, he helped counsel an alcoholic ex-cop turned private detective named Leonard Jenoff. Their time together turned into a friendship of sorts. Eventually, the rabbi started mentioning his marital problems—and how he wanted Jenoff to help make them go away. After considerable discussion, they decided Jenoff would kill Carol at the house and make it look like a robbery gone bad. Jenoff was to get $30,000 for his trouble.

The first attempt was allegedly on October 25, 1994. Jenoff came to the door posing as a deliveryman. Carol answered the door, but her would-be killer lost his nerve and left—though not before asking sheepishly to use the facilities. Carol referred to him thereafter as the "bathroom man."

Not surprisingly, Neulander didn't find this failure funny at all. He ordered Jenoff to try again. This time, Jenoff took backup—Paul Daniels, a fellow substance abuser whom he'd met while staying in a halfway house. He gave him $7,500 to help out with the killing.

Carol Neulander was murdered in her living room by a hired killer she jokingly called "the bathroom man."

On the night of November 1, 1994, they accomplished their mission. Carol was on the phone with her daughter, Rebecca, just seconds before it happened. Their conversation ended with a knock on the door. Carol lightheartedly told her daughter, "Oh, it's the bathroom man," hung up, and went to see what he wanted.

What Jenoff and Daniels wanted, of course, was to kill her. This they accomplished with ruthless speed and great savagery.

At the same time his wife was being slaughtered, Neulander was carefully building his alibi. He diddled around the synagogue, sitting in

Rabbi Fred J. Neulander possessed a legendary gift for gab. But he couldn't talk his way out of a stiff prison sentence for killing his wife.

on a night class and even watching the choir rehearse. Then, at around 9:30 P.M., he went home to "discover" his wife dead on the living room floor. Neulander called emergency services. Among those who heard his plea was his son Matthew, who was studying medicine and riding that evening with an ambulance crew.

Almost immediately, the police started giving the rabbi funny looks. For one thing, when EMTs arrived at the house, they found Neulander wearing an immaculate suit. He didn't have a drop of blood on him. Which meant he hadn't made the slightest move to investigate his wife's injuries or render assistance. People who stumble across the bleeding bodies of loved ones simply don't react that way. Unless the loved one isn't all that loved, or you already know the person is dead.

The man certainly had chutzpah. Just days after the murder, Neulander allegedly paid a portion of the cost of the killing when Jenoff showed up at his house as he sat shivah (mourned, in the Jewish tradition) for Carol. And in August 1997, he had the nerve to preside over the killer's wedding in his own living room, near the spot where his wife died.

By that time, however, the conspiracy had begun to unravel. An unlikely thing had happened. His former associates started having attacks of conscience. In 1995 the other woman, Elaine Soncini, stepped forward to talk about her affair and Neulander's desire to see his wife go away. The rabbi resigned from M'Kor Shalom in February of that same year, admitted his dalliances with congregants shortly there-after, and was then suspended by the Central Conference of American Rabbis. And in 1997, a grand jury that was grinding away at the case learned of an interesting premurder conversation between Neulander and Myron "Pep" Levin. After the two played a racquetball match, the rabbi allegedly told Levin, "I wish I could come home one night and find my wife dead on the floor." Then he asked Levin if he knew of any good hit men. Levin said he didn't.

Finally, in 1998, the cops felt they had enough circumstantial evidence to arrest Neulander for murder. But the really big news came in June 2000. Jenoff, who in his capacity as a private investigator had pretended for years to look for Carol's killer, admitted out of the blue that he and Daniels did it. In exchange for pleading guilty to aggravated manslaughter and robbery, they agreed to testify against their employer.

Neulander was tried twice. The first trial ended in a hung jury, but the second resulted in his conviction. He is, so far as anyone can tell, the first American rabbi to be convicted of a capital crime.

By the end, almost everyone, including his congregation and his own children, abandoned Neulander. About the only thing that stayed faithful was his gift of gab. When he spoke to the jury during the sentencing phase of his trial, he offered a twenty-minute, scripture-filled sermon about the need to do "great things" in life. He said he wanted to help promote literacy in prison. "I beseech you, I importune you, I beg you for that privilege," he said.

All that beseeching and importuning must have worked, because he avoided the death penalty. Instead he got thirty years of hard time.

Neulander also, to the horror of many in the courtroom, said that he had loved and *still* loved his wife.

If so, he certainly he had a funny way of showing it.

THE GAME OF DEATH

A macabre tale of what can happen when today's kids put down their iPods and Game Boys and "make their own fun."

One hopes that nationally renowned DNA researcher Robert Schwartz didn't live long enough to contemplate the irony of his own demise. A man who spent his life working on the leading edge of technology was cut down in his own kitchen by an assailant straight out of the Dark Ages—a sword-wielding young man who believed he was serving as knight errant for a damsel in distress. A damsel who happened to be Schwartz's own daughter, Clara.

The world didn't become aware of his grisly end until December 10, 2001. It was a Monday, and Schwartz, fifty-seven, was overdue at the Center for Innovative Technology in Herndon, Virginia, where he worked. His office mates phoned one of his neighbors, who walked over to his old farmhouse, located in the Washington, D.C., suburban town of Hamilton, to check things out. The neighbor found Schwartz facedown in a pool of his own blood, stabbed dozens of times.

Investigators didn't have to look far for the bungling perpetrators. Neighbors reported that at the approximate time of the murder, two teenage boys and a girl had arrived at the house by car. When they tried to leave, they realized their vehicle had become stuck in the mud. In a case of supremely bad judgment, they called a tow truck to extract it. They even gave the driver their correct names and addresses, making it easy for the police to round up Kyle Hulbert, eighteen; Michael Paul Pfohl, twenty-one; and Katherine Inglis, nineteen. All three were friends of Clara Schwartz, and all three shared their stories almost as soon as they were taken in. It was an account as pitiful as it was horrible.

Clara, as it turned out, lived a double life. On the surface she was a bright, twenty-one-year-old computer science major at James Madison University. But intimates said she was also a sullen kid who dressed in Goth clothes and seemed fascinated by Dungeons & Dragons–style role-playing games. Hulbert, Pfohl, and Inglis were all gaming buddies of hers. To them, Clara had intimated that Schwartz abused her (an unsubstantiated charge). Hulbert, who had been diagnosed with paranoid schizophrenia and institutionalized several times, took all of this to heart. Which, apparently, is exactly what Clara hoped he would do.

From top to bottom: Clara Schwartz, Katherine Inglis, Michael Paul Pfohl, and Kyle Hulbert.

This type of fantasy gaming made a particularly poor hobby for Hulbert, with his already tenuous grip on reality. However, he was perfect for what Clara had in mind. She met him at a Renaissance festival in Crownsville, Maryland, and poured out the story that her father abused her and wanted her dead. To Hulbert, caught up in role-playing dramatics, Clara became his damsel in distress.

He was convinced that Schwartz intended to kill Clara during an upcoming family vacation to the Virgin Islands. So he decided to act first. On December 8, he had Pfohl (who knew what was about to happen) and Inglis (who didn't) drive him to the Schwartz house in Hamilton. There, he confronted Clara's father and killed him savagely with a samurai sword, stabbing him dozens of times. Afterward he called Clara to let her know he had "done the job."

Police put together a more complete picture when they reviewed the coded e-mails Clara unwisely saved on her computer. In them she discussed her fear that her father (whom she referred to as OG, short for "old guy") had homicidal intentions, and her desire to beat him to the punch. It was also learned that Hulbert wasn't her first choice of cat's-paw. Earlier she had convinced another boy to get involved in a role-playing game of her own design in which she played a character called Lord Chaos. Her opponent was a character called Old Guy who was supposedly her father, and the boy played the assassin. Reportedly, the boy dropped out when he finally realized he was being prepped to actually kill the real-life Old Guy.

The trials of the defendants were filled with arcane references to vampires, sorcery, spells, and swordplay. But all that really mattered was one dead scientist. Inglis, who cooperated with prosecutors and hadn't had any knowledge of what was going to happen, got twelve months. Clara was convicted of first-degree murder and sentenced to forty-eight years. Hulbert, who pleaded guilty to first-degree murder, was sentenced to life without parole. Pfohl got twenty-one years and four months.

Presumably they'll all have lots of free time to play games while sweating it out in the pen.

SHREDS OF EVIDENCE

One of the aspiring suburban murderer's most vexing problems is what to do with the victim's body. There's the traditional option of rolling the whole mess up in a tarp, dropping it in a car trunk, and taking the not-so-dearly departed on a one-way trip to the nearest forest, swamp, or landfill. Closer-to-home solutions include crawl space internment, walling up the corpse in a convenient basement nook, or incorporating it into, say, a new concrete patio or driveway.

When disposing of a dead body, a homicidal husband should never let the chips fall where they may.

That's what makes the scheme hatched by airline pilot Richard Crafts so interesting. He found a novel way to make the corpse of his murdered wife disappear. Or most of it, anyway. All he needed to accomplish this feat was a commercial-grade wood chipper—and the barren soul of a sociopath.

That was Crafts all over. His wife was a beautiful Danish stewardess named Helle, whom he married in 1975. The couple had three children

and made enough money between them to enjoy a comfortable suburban lifestyle. They resided in a ranch house in the picturesque western
Connecticut town of Newton. But all wasn't well at the Crafts abode—
or even normal. Helle told friends that her husband beat her, and that
she knew he'd cheated on her for years with numerous women. In
1986, she'd apparently had enough. She hired a divorce attorney and a
private detective to look into her mate's activities.

She needed a PI because her husband made a point of concealing
his movements. He would often pack his bags and vanish for days
without saying where he was going or what he planned to do. But the
parts of his life that Helle did know about were disconcerting enough.
For one thing, he owned a substantial and ever-increasing arsenal of
guns, from revolvers to high-powered rifles. And for another, he nursed
an oddball fetish for police work. It got so bad that Crafts, who as a
pilot pulled down a very high salary, took a low-paying part-time job
as a police officer in the nearby town of Southbury. He also attended
expensive programs on police procedure that he paid for himself, and
he even fitted out a 1985 Ford Crown Victoria (the same model the
Connecticut state police used) as a faux cop car, complete with radios,
lights, and other gear.

But though Crafts dressed like a cop, he thought like a thug. And
he clearly wasn't pleased with his wife's attempts to extricate herself
from their marriage. On November 17, 1986, he took delivery on a
large-capacity freezer. At about the same time, he spent $900 to rent
some heavy-duty equipment. Then, on the morning of November 19,
he awakened his kids' live-in au pair and told her to get the children
ready for a trip to his sister's house in Westport—even though an
early-winter blizzard raged outside. Crafts drove them all to his sister's,
then departed almost immediately. That evening when he returned,
his kids asked where their mom was. He said he didn't know.

And that was the last anyone saw of Helle Crafts.

But though she was out of sight, she wasn't out of mind. The private
detective she'd hired began to complain to the local constabulary
about her sudden disappearance, as did her many friends. They said

Helle told them that if she ever vanished, to suspect foul play. And they also pointed out that Crafts was constantly concocting new stories to explain his wife's absence.

Slowly, police interest grew. On Christmas Day, 1986, while Crafts and his kids were in Florida on vacation, the Newton police executed a search warrant on his house at 5 Newfield Lane. The cops, who entered through a rear window, found the place in complete disarray, with dishes stacked in the kitchen and mattresses and furniture strewn everywhere. After a careful search, they seized dozens of pieces of potential evidence, from the arsenal of guns to hand towels with suspicious-looking stains.

Extensive testing showed that particular spots in the house, along with some pieces of linen, contained traces of O-negative blood— Helle's blood type. Although authorities were more or less convinced that something bad had happened, they couldn't say what. And they weren't any closer to finding the victim.

The trail got warmer in the coming days. Unfortunately, it didn't

Wife-murderer Richard Crafts gets hauled off to jail after police piece together—literally—the evidence.

lead to a very good place. Investigators poring over Crafts's charge card receipts uncovered the $900 tool rental bill, which turned out to be for a heavy-duty wood chipper. It was an unusual item to need in the middle of winter. Then, on December 30, police located a utility worker named Joseph Hine who had been plowing snow late on the night of November 20. He said that while traveling down River Road, he spotted a wood chipper attached to a U-Haul truck. It was parked next to a stretch of the Housatonic River called Lake Zoar.

All the bits of evidence came together to create an extremely disturbing picture. The cops paid a visit to the spot where Hine saw the chipper and looked around. They found wood chips, all right, but other things as well. Most incriminating, they located scraps of shredded mail. One piece even included a name and address: Miss Helle L. Crafts, 5 Newfield Lane, Newton, Connecticut.

Within hours the area was crawling with search teams. A more detailed look at the shoreline turned up several other pieces of Helle's mail, along with several pieces of Helle herself, such as bone fragments and strands of hair. The bits were shipped off to the state's forensic crime lab for identification, along with the wood chipper itself, which was tracked down at the tool rental agency.

Meanwhile, back at the river, police divers and shore teams probed the icy water for two weeks. Investigators eventually turned up a discarded chainsaw blade, along with more bits of Helle Crafts, including two teeth, a bit of finger, a fingernail, three ounces of tissue, and 2,660 strands of blond hair.

On January 11 at 9:00 P.M., police showed up at Richard Crafts's house with an arrest warrant. They called him on the phone and told him to step outside. Perhaps not grasping that the jig was up, he initially replied, "I'm tired. I'll take care of it in the morning." It took several more conversations to convince him that the small army of Connecticut state troopers and other officers ringing his property weren't going to leave without him. Finally, at about 12:30 that night, Crafts surrendered and was taken away in handcuffs for arraignment.

Police figured it went down like this: At the crack of dawn on

November 19, Crafts crept up on his wife in their bedroom and beat her to death, quickly and quietly. Then, while the rest of his family slept, he lugged the corpse down to the basement and jammed it in the big, new freezer he'd just purchased. Next he woke up the au pair and the kids and told them they were going to his sister's house in Westport. After he dropped them off, he returned home, retrieved his wife's frozen corpse from the freezer, and used a chainsaw to cut it into several chipper-friendly sized pieces. These he wrapped in plastic garbage bags and put back into the freezer. Late the next night, he took them and his big wood chipper to the banks of Lake Zoar. He positioned the unit as close to the water as possible, dropped the pieces of the former Mrs. Crafts in its business end, and watched as her mortal remains sprayed out over the river.

For his trouble, Crafts was sentenced to ninety-nine years in state prison. That's plenty of time to think about the fact that he almost got away with it. Too bad for him that his wife had so many friends. Even after she was gone, they refused to let her be forgotten.

THE HOUSE OF HORROR

Some creepy, old domiciles harbor things far more lethal than ghosts.

Brooklyn native Ron DeFeo Sr. probably figure he'd "arrived" both financially and socially when he purchased a home for his family in suburban Long Island. It must have seemed as if he, his wife, Louise, and their five children had escaped into a paradise of big lawns and white picket fences.

They couldn't have been more wrong. Little did they know that their Shangri La in the sticks would soon become an international symbol for terror—a terror so palpable that, decades after the awful events that overtook them there, the mere sight of their former abode can still unnerve the timid.

Of course, at the time the DeFeos purchased it, the two-story structure with the spacious attic didn't give off a dangerous or fearful vibe. But the same couldn't be said of the family's eldest child, Ronald "Butch" DeFeo Jr. A sullen kid, he'd been picked on by his father from an early age. As he got older he got more violent—and more scary. By his teen years he was using everything from alcohol to heroin and dabbling in petty crime as well. Once, when his father and mother were having one of their frequent, violent arguments, Butch grabbed a 12-gauge shotgun, popped in a single shell, pointed the weapon at his father's face, and pulled the trigger. When, for some reason, the gun didn't go off, he simply walked out of the room.

It was a bloodless preview of a very bloody nightmare to come. For years, Butch had enjoyed a cushy job at the family's Brooklyn Buick dealership, where he received a generous weekly stipend for doing busywork—when he felt like it. A couple of weeks before all hell broke loose, Butch was asked to deposit $1,800 in cash and $20,000 in checks at the bank. Instead, he hit upon a not-very-clever idea. He arranged for a friend to "rob" him in exchange for a cut of the loot.

On the appointed day, Butch and another accomplice from the dealership returned to inform his father that they'd been relieved of their money by a robber while sitting in their car at a stoplight. DeFeo Sr. didn't buy it and flew into a rage. The cops didn't buy it either. Butch didn't help his case much. From the start, he was angry and uncooperative with his questioners. He even refused to look at mug shots to help identify the person who allegedly robbed him. This was extremely odd behavior for a crime victim but pretty standard for a suspect, which is what both DeFeo Sr. and the police soon believed Butch to be.

The old man confronted his son in his usual, low-key way. "You've got the devil on your back," he supposedly screamed at him. Butch responded by telling his dad that he wanted to kill him.

He made good on his vow on the night of November 14, 1974. Butch was the only member of his family to have his own room, which gave him both a measure of privacy and a place to store his small arsenal of weapons. Late that night, after everyone else had gone to bed, he pulled out a .35-caliber Marlin rifle and padded silently to his parents' bedroom. First he fired two shots into DeFeo Sr., then two more rounds into his mother.

Next, he moved on to the room where his brothers, Mark and John, slept. Incredibly, the sound of the four rifle shots from their parents' room hadn't roused them. Standing between their beds, Butch fired one round into each, killing them. Next it was on to the room occupied by his sisters, Dawn and Allison. Again, Butch killed them both with one shot each. Murdering his entire family took about fifteen minutes.

What came next was almost as horrible. With the killings done, the murderer calmly started preparing his alibi. Butch showered, dressed in fresh clothes, then packed the rifle and his blood-spattered shirt and pants in a pillowcase. He tossed the mess into his car, drove into Brooklyn, and ditched the evidence in a storm drain. Then he went back to Long Island and reported for work at the Buick dealership at 6:00 A.M., as if nothing had happened.

That day he continued fine-tuning his alibi. He made a great show of calling home, then remarking that no one answered. Around noon he

For killing his family, Ronald "Butch" DeFeo Jr. will probably spend the rest of his life as a guest of the New York State Department of Corrections.

left the dealership and visited his sometimes girlfriend, Sherry Klein. In her presence, he again called the house, then complained theatrically that while he knew someone must be there, no one answered. He and Klein hit the mall together, where they ran into another friend, Bobby Kelske. Butch served up his now-familiar "everyone's home but no one picks up the phone" spiel once more.

He spent the rest of the evening boozing and doing heroin. That evening he hooked up with Kelske at a bar called Henry's and announced with great fanfare that he was headed home to find out why he couldn't reach anyone. A few minutes later he returned, out of breath, saying that there'd been a massacre at his house. The bar patrons piled into a car and drove to the scene, discovered the victims, and called the local cops.

When the first police cruiser arrived, Butch was the picture of grief, crying and shouting, "My mother and father are dead." And dead they were, as the police soon confirmed. In an initial interview, Butch blamed the killings on a local mafia hit man who he said had had a run-in with his family.

Not surprisingly, the story unraveled like a cheap suit. Almost immediately, investigators discovered a box for a .35-caliber Marlin rifle in the house. Butch had tossed the gun but had forgotten about its container. Soon he was read his rights and given a lengthy grilling. Faced with this new development, he violated the cardinal rule of the guilty—stick to your story. Butch began blabbing about being kidnapped by the hit man and an accomplice (whom he couldn't even vaguely describe). The police egged him on, occasionally pointing out the numerous gaps of logic and evidence in his story. Finally the killer collapsed under the weight of his own lies and confessed.

Butch went to trial in October 1975. Thanks in part to the defendant's performance on the witness stand, in which he actually threatened the prosecutor's life, he got six counts of second-degree murder and a sentence of twenty-five years to (far more likely) life. Today he remains a mandatory guest of the New York State Department of Corrections.

But that wasn't the end of the story. It was only the prelude.

Police pay a call to the soon-to-be-infamous DeFeo household.

While the DeFeo family had been annihilated, their house remained. It was a vaguely sinister-looking structure with a pair of oddly shaped attic windows that looked like eyes. At least that's what they looked like to George and Kathy Lutz, who purchased the place at roughly the same time that Butch was settling into his prison cell. But they didn't stay very long. "George and Kathy Lutz moved into 112 Ocean Avenue on December 18," says the account written of the alleged supernatural horrors they encountered there. "Twenty-eight days later, they fled in terror."

The suburban house at 112 Ocean Avenue is located in Amityville, New York. And the book documenting the Lutz's stay there is called *The Amityville Horror*. Of course, more than a few people contend that the Lutz family made up their story. But whatever one thinks of the tale they told about their time in that infamous Amityville house, there's no doubt that it pales before the real terror that happened there.

PART

HELLISH COMMUTES

Blighted locales and unnerving driving
distractions that give new urgency to the
popular phrase "Don't go there"

ROADSIDE ASSISTANCE

Next to tales of ghostly hitchhikers, one of the most widely circulated supernatural stories concerns a group of schoolchildren who, "many years ago," were killed when a train collided with their school bus, which was stalled on a section of railroad track. The event is supposedly commemorated in a nearby subdivision, which was allegedly built at about the same time as the accident. The streets are all named after the dead kids.

A gaggle of ghostly children proves it's always unwise to get caught on the wrong side of the tracks.

And now, the story goes, if you park your car on the tracks where it happened and put the car in neutral, a pack of invisible tots will push your ride out of danger. Even more creepy, if you dust the back of the car with talcum powder, after you roll off the rails you'll be able to see ghostly handprints on the trunk.

The story seems as implausible as it is entertaining. What makes it even more astounding is that it contains a grain—a very small grain—

of truth. It turns out the original mother of all child-haunted railroad crossings is set on the southern edge of San Antonio, near a tiny suburban neighborhood where the streets do indeed bear names such as Nancy Carole Way, Cindy Sue Way, Laura Lee Way, and Shane Road. Head west on Shane, and you'll very quickly hit a rail line. *The rail line.*

If you pull up to the eastern side and look across the tracks, it seems as if the road ahead slopes gently uphill. Which makes what comes next even more disturbing. Throw the car into neutral and it will roll eerily forward, over the tracks, and back onto the road. And if you conduct the talcum powder test, there's a decent chance you may find prints on your trunk at the end of the adventure.

Not surprisingly, this railroad crossing is an extremely popular spot with teenagers—particularly around Halloween, when lines of cars wait patiently for a chance to roll across the tracks. Indeed, one wonders if the ghost kids ever get tired. One also wonders, given the stupidity and inherent danger of goofing around on railroad tracks for any reason, whether the toiling tots haven't been joined over the decades by a few unobservant thrill seekers. One would think those invisible, car-pushing grade-schoolers would serve as a warning.

Sadly for ghost lovers, there's a logical explanation for almost all of this. A few years ago a San Antonio TV station hired surveyors to examine the road. They found that in spite of appearances (or a common misperception), the grade slopes downhill rather than up. So a car placed in neutral could roll over the tracks from east to west naturally, without any ghostly assistance. Even more telling, extensive research turned up no record of a school bus crash at that spot.

There's even a perfectly reasonable, perfectly boring explanation for the handprints. When would-be ghost hunters spray their trunks with talc, the material is soaked up by oil from any handprints that might be there already, casting them into sharp relief. As anyone who has taken a criminology course, or even watched an episode of *Law & Order*, already knows, this is exactly how the cops dust for fingerprints.

And by the way, the streets in the nearby neighborhood aren't named after dead children. They're named after the suburban developer's own kids.

Not that true believers can't find some wiggle room. The TV station that tried to debunk the story admitted that while it couldn't locate any hard evidence of a school bus accident, records from earlier decades were so spotty that something might have been missed. Even more telling, not long ago the teenage daughter of Andy and Debi Chesney brought back a tangible souvenir from her trip to the tracks. After she and her friends took the customary roll over the rails, she shot some pictures to commemorate the event. But when the roll was developed, the Chesneys were disconcerted by one particular picture. Down in the left corner was a transparent, child-sized shape.

It looks, to some, like the outline of a kid carrying a teddy bear.

RESURRECTION MARY, QUITE CONTRARY

Commuters who drive down Archer Avenue in suburban Chicago don't make a habit of picking up strangers. Of course, giving rides to hitchhikers is never a good idea, but it's a particularly terrible one here. Especially if the pedestrian in question is the apparition of a young woman in a white dress. Not that she's all that dangerous. She's not out for blood or to steal your soul. All she really wants is a lift—and, perhaps, to frighten you silly. According to local legend, she's wandered this same strip of blacktop for some eighty years. That single-mindedness, along with a healthy blast of Windy City publicity, has made her one of the spirit world's biggest celebrities: Resurrection Mary, queen of the ghostly hitchhikers.

No, you can't drive the cute female hitchhiker on Chicago's Archer Avenue home. Metaphysically speaking, you can't get there from here.

In America and Europe, tales of such roadside specters are a dime a dozen. They're so common that almost every community with a bit of lonely pavement has its own. The standard legend goes something like this: A driver sees a young girl walking on the shoulder and offers her a ride. She accepts and directs him to her "home." But when the driver arrives at the address, his passenger suddenly vanishes. He later learns that a girl matching her description did live there, but died years ago when she was hit by a car while walking exactly the same section of highway where he picked her up.

The story is a classic urban legend. It's so ancient and widespread that centuries ago, one could hear versions involving specters who tried to flag down coaches and lone horsemen.

But just as there are numberless Elvis impersonators but only one Elvis, there are hundreds of phantom hitchhiker stories, but only one Resurrection Mary. Sometime in the 1930s, Archer Avenue drivers started sighting a young girl who tried to jump on the running boards of their cars, then suddenly vanished. As the years passed, the tales got taller. Some witnesses claimed to have actually given rides to a woman in white, only to see her disappear into thin air as they passed a vast graveyard called Resurrection Cemetery. Others went even further. Occasionally young men stated that they danced with a strange girl at the O Henry Ballroom, located a few clicks down the road. Afterward, they drove their dance partner "home." But as soon as they passed the entrance to Resurrection Cemetery, the boys found themselves alone.

Inevitably, an elaborate biography was invented for the apparition. Mary (no one knows where the name originated) supposedly met her doom after a night spent dancing at the O Henry with her boyfriend. Late in the evening, they got into an argument, and she stormed out. She tried to walk home along Archer Avenue, but was struck and killed by a hit-and-run driver. Her parents buried her at Resurrection Cemetery in a white dress.

The story is much, much too good to be literally true. Investigations have shown that while there are a couple of intriguing "Mary" candidates buried at Resurrection Cemetery, their lives and deaths don't jibe very well with the spectral hitchhiker's bio.

None of which stops people from looking for her—or keeps new reports from cropping up.

Not surprisingly, the folks who run the three-hundred-acre (121 hectare), immaculately kept Resurrection Cemetery would dearly love to see the entire story vanish into thin air, just as Mary so often does. After all, having a restless spirit reportedly wandering the grounds can't be great publicity for a place whose sole reason for existence is to provide eternal peace to its residents. But there's not much chance of relief, given the events that supposedly took place on the night of August 10, 1976. That evening, a driver passing the cemetery allegedly spotted a girl in a white dress standing at the locked entrance, grasping the gate's iron bars in her hands as she looked out. Figuring someone had been trapped after hours, he reported it to the police.

The cops found no one. But what they did find at the spot where the "girl" supposedly grasped the gate, were two bars bent outward, with a handprint embedded in each. And this time it was no tall tale. Anyone who wanted to (and plenty of people did) could see the gnarled metal for themselves. Cemetery management quickly offered a perfectly rational-sounding explanation: A truck had backed into the gate and damaged it. Repairmen tried to straighten the bars by heating them with a blowtorch and pushing them back into place, inadvertently creating what looked like handprints in the metal.

Still, the cemetery remains a macabre tourist attraction that continues to draw the curious today—in spite of several coats of paint and further repair attempts. Visitors are advised to stop by during the day and not to linger after dark. And try to avoid rush hour. Because as Resurrection Mary knows, the traffic on Archer Avenue can be murder.

CLOSE ENCOUNTERS OF THE WORST KIND

Remember the scene from *Close Encounters of the Third Kind* in which police cruisers take off on a high-speed, semihumorous pursuit of ground-skimming UFOs? Believe it or not, this was based on an actual encounter from 1966. But the real chase, and the life-changing repercussions it held for the many men who conducted it, were no laughing matter.

A pack of cops stumbled into the ultimate chase when they tried to pull over a UFO.

It began at around 5 in the morning on April 17, on the shoulder of Route 224 in Portage County, Ohio, just south of Cleveland. Deputy sheriff Dale Spaur and mounted deputy Wilbur "Barney" Neff had parked their police cruiser and were warily approaching an abandoned car they'd spotted on the side of the road. But suddenly, a large flying saucer with bright lights rose out of the woods behind them. Spaur noticed it first as it levitated to a height of perhaps one hundred feet (30 m).

He quickly alerted his partner. The two stood slack-jawed, staring as the craft moved toward them, so brightly illuminated that it turned the predawn murkiness into day. "The only thing, the only sound in the whole area was a hum," Spaur said later.

Regaining their composure, the cops jumped back into their car and watched as the UFO veered off toward the east. Spaur reported what had happened to his dispatcher and was told to pursue.

And so the chase was on. Actually, so long as the flying saucer stayed close to the ground and kept a reasonable speed, it was a breeze to tail. It was so bright, Spaur said, that "it'd make your eyes water." Still, they pushed their cruiser to the limit to keep up. The UFO ambled east at what, for it, must have been a leisurely pace. But the cops had to drive at more than one hundred miles an hour (160 km/h) just to stay in the general vicinity.

As dawn broke, the two men got a better look at their quarry. It was reportedly silver, with some sort of tail fin or projection at the rear—or at what the gumshoes assumed was the rear. It seemed to be about forty feet (12 m) wide and eighteen feet (5.4 m) high. As the minutes passed, they highballed through jurisdiction after jurisdiction, keeping up a running commentary on their radio. In East Palestine, Ohio, an officer named H. Wayne Huston listened in, then parked at an intersection he knew they'd have to pass. Shortly thereafter he saw the UFO glide overhead, followed moments later by Portage County's finest in their severely overtaxed squad car. Huston fell in behind them and joined the chase.

The pursuit ended in Conway, Pennsylvania, when Spaur, low on gas, pulled over to ask a local cop for assistance. While the officer was on his radio seeking instructions, Huston pulled up and joined the party. The UFO, obligingly, hovered nearby in plain sight, as if waiting for the game of tag to resume.

But it wasn't to be. The officers heard chatter on their car radios about Air Force jets being scrambled to investigate. Soon afterward they thought they saw fighters approaching. That, apparently, was too much for whomever piloted the flying saucer. The craft suddenly shot straight up, out of sight.

But Spaur would see it again. Once more in the real world, and endlessly in his nightmares.

The official investigation into the affair, viewed from the distance of four decades, looks like a by-the-book whitewash. Police chief Gerald Buchert of Mantua told the *Cleveland Plain Dealer* that he took a photo of the thing as it passed his house. But he also said that someone from the Air Force told him not to give the image to anyone. The military denied scrambling the interceptors that seemed to flush the UFO. Finally, in the famous Project Blue Book, the entire affair was pooh-poohed as a case of mistaken identity. The flying saucer, which was so bright it cast shadows, was dismissed as a misidentification of Venus, or of a satellite, or perhaps of both.

None of this washed with the men who had risked their lives driving at breakneck speeds down dark roads to keep an eye on the thing. "We were close, closer than I ever want to be again," Spaur told the *Plain Dealer*. "I know nobody's going to believe it, but it's true."

He was dead right about the "nobody's going to believe it" part. But what he couldn't know was that his game of tag with the harmless-seeming flying saucer would ruin his life.

Within six months of the sighting, Spaur lost his job and his marriage and was hovering on the edge of destitution. And he wasn't the only one hitting rock bottom. The Pennsylvania policeman to whom he'd turned for assistance clammed up so tight he actually had his phone removed. Officer H. Wayne Huston, who brought up the rear during the pursuit, turned in his badge, changed his name to Harold W. Huston, moved to Seattle, and became a bus driver. Even Neff, who rode shotgun with Spaur that fateful morning, wouldn't say a word. "He never talks about it anymore," his wife, Jackelyne, told the *Plain Dealer*. "Once he told me, 'If that thing landed in my back yard, I wouldn't tell a soul.' He's been through a wringer."

The cherry on top of the cover-up sundae was provided by Buchert, who had taken a photo of the craft from his porch. "I'd rather not talk about it," he told the *Plain Dealer* later. "It's something that should be forgotten . . . left alone. I saw something, but I don't know what it was."

This is the sort of talk that sends conspiracy theorists into blogging frenzies. But the truth is, witnesses weren't silenced or ruined by mysterious Men in Black or ruthless government agents. Their fellow citizens did the job. All were mercilessly ribbed about the incident and painted either as gullible morons or as total wack jobs.

Spaur, who led the pursuit and, afterward, exuberantly shot off his mouth about it to the papers, took the most flack. Reporters from around the world harassed him, as did legions of UFO enthusiasts. Though the now-well-known phrase hadn't been coined yet, he was getting his fifteen minutes of fame. But the glaring spotlight fried him. When his estranged father called him after years of silence, it was to ask about the UFO. And when he sought solace at a church, he was introduced to the congregation as the guy who chased the flying saucer. "Everything changed," he sullenly told the *Plain Dealer*. "I still don't really know what happened. But suddenly, it was as though everybody owned me. And I no longer had anything for myself. My wife, my home, my children. They all seemed to fade away."

Incredibly, the one thing that didn't fade away was the UFO itself. In June 1966, right before he quit police work, Spaur saw the saucer in broad daylight while driving down I-80 outside Cleveland. The last thing his department wanted was another spaceman flap, so the staff created an on-air radio code to use if the visitor ever returned. The silver ship was to be called "Floyd," which was Spaur's middle name.

On that day, the soon-to-be-ex-deputy whispered, "Floyd's here with me," into his radio. Then he pulled off onto the shoulder, lit a smoke, and stared resolutely at his floorboard for a quarter of an hour. When he looked out the window again, Floyd was gone.

So in the end, the UFO that Spaur had so doggedly tailed wound up tailing him.

But one other intriguing thing happened on that strange morning—something that was largely forgotten in the crush of events. Remember the car the two cops were checking when the UFO first rose up out of the trees? Just before all hell broke loose, the officers noticed that it was filled with communications equipment. On the side was a curious triangle framing a bolt of lightning. Above this were the sinister words "Seven Steps to Hell."

When police finally returned to the spot, the car had vanished. Did it have something to do with the flying saucer? Perhaps, or perhaps not. At this late date, no one will ever know. All it is, and all it will ever be, is one more strange footnote to a very strange, very sad encounter.

DEATH TAKES A HOLIDAY INN

Any bed-and-breakfast worth its doilies claims to be haunted, it seems. A ghost on the grounds is part of the ambience, right along with the Victorian-style furnishings and blueberry scones. Touting the occasional spirit visitation is just one more way these tiny operations can set themselves apart from the "big boys." After all, you'd never expect to find something so macabre at a Holiday Inn.

Unless it happens to be the Holiday Inn Grand Island.

This palatial establishment,

This place has all the amenities, including a gym, turn-down service, strange cold spots, and a spectral entity with no respect for Do Not Disturb signs.

located on the outskirts of Buffalo, New York, offers a little something extra to some of its guests—and we're not talking about turndown service or a free mint on the pillow. Let's just say that if you happen to stay in room 422, you'll never be alone. Because while this particular

Room 422 at the Holiday Inn Grand Island may be smoke-free,
but it isn't ghost-free.

nonsmoking space is occasionally vacant, it's never really empty.

The Grand Island in general, and room 422 in particular, is haunted
by what the staff believes is the mischievous spirit of a little girl
they've taken to calling Tanya. According to a so-far-unsubstantiated
local legend, she's the ghost of a child who was killed in a fire at a
house where the hotel now stands. These days she occupies herself by
raising good-natured mayhem among the guests and employees.
Housekeepers report hearing disembodied giggles and what sounds
like a child running noisily (and invisibly) down the halls. Apparently
Tanya also likes to jump on beds, and on one occasion she snatched
all the cleaning products off a maid's cart—then put them all back
before the flummoxed woman returned with a bemused supervisor.
Some staffers (who must either have nerves of steel or really, really
need their jobs) also report hearing a child call their names—a child
who is nowhere to be found.

The visitations can be particularly intense around room 422.

Allegedly, even those who simply walk past its door can sometimes sense a ghostly presence. Cold seems to ooze out into the hallway, and cameras act up in the area, producing pictures containing strange, illuminated orbs that are invisible to the naked eye.

The weird part (well, one of the weird parts) is that Tanya's presence hasn't hurt business at the Grand Island one bit. Especially not for room 422, which has become a tourist attraction of sorts. "People get kind of angry when they find out it's occupied," says one employee. Guests have so few reservations about staying with the ghost that reservations are required (usually weeks in advance) if you wish to enjoy the privilege.

If you want to meet Tanya, patience is a virtue. You may be in a hurry, but she's got all the time in the world.

THE DEAD ZONE

Everyone who lives in the area knows that getting trapped on Orlando's Interstate 4 during rush hour can be a nightmare. You'd better have a full tank of gas, because at peak times the combination of clueless tourists trying to get back to their hotels and harassed commuters trying to reach their homes often congeals into total gridlock.

But there's one bit of I-4 that's worth taking care on—or, even better, steering clear of—even if you're the only car on the highway. *Especially* if you're the only car on the highway. The stretch of blacktop sits just north of Orlando, in Seminole County, at the south end of the St. Johns River bridge. This section of roadway is only a quarter of a mile (400 m) long, yet it's allegedly the scene of an extraordinarily large number of traffic accidents. Almost as unnerving, cell phones and radios tend to act up around here, either filling with static or, sometimes, picking up strange voices.

Don't complain if you lose cell phone service on this haunted Florida highway. Just be happy if that's all you lose.

Defiling a tiny cemetery created grave problems for this innocuous
stretch of Sunshine State blacktop.

The area is the site of so many odd occurrences that locals call it the Dead Zone. What makes this one tiny stretch of a state-spanning highway so problematic? It all began during its construction in 1960, when a graveyard was obliterated to make room for the project. The cemetery contained the graves of four family members who had lived in a Roman Catholic–sponsored settlement called St. Joseph's Colony. But the little town, vexed by disease and natural disaster, failed to thrive. By the time the four succumbed to yellow fever around 1885, the colony was so depleted that there wasn't even a priest available to deliver last rites.

After the passing of the colony, the territory was turned over to agriculture. The farmer who worked the ground steadfastly left the graves alone, so that the little plots formed an island in the middle of his cultivated land. Locals came to call the spot—which at that time wasn't known for any ghostly manifestations—the Field of the Dead. And that's how things stayed until, in 1960, the parcel was purchased by the state of Florida for I-4.

The landmark was reportedly noted by surveyors, but project planners considered the graves of no historical significance and not worth saving. Shortly thereafter, the Field of the Dead vanished under the mountain of fill dirt needed to build up the new highway bed. Interestingly, some say that at the very time the dirt was being mounded up over the graves, Hurricane Donna—one of the worst storms ever to hit central Florida— pummeled the state, its eye passing almost directly over the work zone. The resulting damage and flooding set the project back by months.

If this was some sort of sign, it went unheeded. Soon the graves disappeared for good beneath I-4's eastbound lanes.

But just because we can't see them doesn't mean they aren't still there—or that their occupants aren't upset. Over the years, numerous reports of strange occurrences along the roadway have trickled in. They range from thick clouds that dart across traffic lanes with supernatural speed to peculiar late-night ghost lights to uncanny cell phone interference—including unwanted messages from what one witness called "voices of the dead."

And, of course, there are all those accidents.

If anything, the ghosts should be even more riled these days. Over the last couple of years the road was widened and improved, subjecting the area's undead inhabitants to the rumble of heavy machinery and yet another dose of fill dirt. There's no word as to whether this has made things better or worse for commuters and tourists using the Dead Zone. But just to be on the safe side, if you find yourself heading out of Orlando on I-4, shut off your cell phone and keep both hands on the wheel.

THE PARKWAY PHANTOM

A roadside demon gives travelers one more reason to steer clear of the so-called Garden State.

Motorists seeking the path of least resistance through New Jersey often select the Garden State Parkway, a 173-mile (280 km) length of asphalt and concrete that runs the length of the state, linking New York City in the north to Delaware in the south. Travel this route, and you'll witness an almost impossibly dramatic change of scenery, from a densely populated, urbanized landscape in the north to sparsely settled wilderness in the south.

But this isn't just any wilderness. This is the fabled Pine Barrens—a land of swamps, scrub, and forest that for hundreds of years has been the home to numerous reports of (hopefully) mythical monsters. Among many other things, this blighted land hosts the fabled Jersey Devil. This beast, which stands taller than a man and possesses bat wings and the head of a horse, has been reported to have plagued area residents for centuries.

A bizarre entity plagues drivers on the Garden State Parkway.

But the Jersey Devil isn't the only apparition working this bit of territory. One of its less-famous associates is called the Parkway Phantom. As can be guessed from the name, it takes a particular (and decidedly unhealthy) interest in folks motoring down the Garden State Parkway.

Two different kinds of encounters with the entity have been described: the confusing, annoying kind, and the superscary kind. In the former, drivers report spotting a very tall, very skinny man wearing an old-fashioned long topcoat and standing next to a disabled car. He seems to be trying to flag down help, but the only part of his body that moves is one outstretched hand. Should anyone respond to his plea and pull over, all they find is empty space. The phantom, and the car, simply vanish.

The superscary kind is quite a bit more intense. Witnesses report seeing a tall, lean man in contemporary but seedy-looking clothes. But instead of standing stock-still beside the road, he waves both hands over his head in a highly agitated, peculiar manner—a manner that some have likened to "a strange football cheer."

And then things get really nasty. The phantom, still waving, steps resolutely onto the highway and into the path of oncoming traffic.

Drivers report having to swerve wildly to avoid collisions. One rattled commuter even described the encounter to a toll booth collector. Apparently the collector merely smiled, as if she'd heard the same story many times before.

This apparition operates strictly at night and confines its activity to the northbound side of the parkway—specifically, a roughly eight-mile (13 km) span bracketing Exit 82. Could it all be a hoax? Perhaps, but if so, the hoaxer picked a really bad place to have his sick fun. This stretch of parkway is close to the Toms River Barracks of the New Jersey State Police. Presumably, if some local moron was playing in traffic, they would have caught him. But so far no one has been apprehended—and no one's offered an explanation for the large number of accidents along this stretch of road.

Perhaps the best course of action is to not stop for strangers. And while you're at it, don't brake for them, either.

OUR LADY OF THE SAVINGS AND LOAN

A blessed vision creates the (holy) mother of all traffic jams.

Pity the poor Clearwater, Florida, office drones who were forced to take the U.S. 19 corridor to work back in 1996. The six-lane road can be crawling chaos on good days, but during the holiday season that year it was brought to a virtual halt. Cursing the source of the obstruction wasn't an option, unless you wanted a one-way, express ticket to Hell. Because, according to true believers, the person holding up traffic was none other than the Virgin Mary herself.

Or, rather, her ghostly apparition. It all began innocently enough, when on December 17 a customer visiting the Seminole Finance Corporation building (a boxlike affair fronted on all sides with mirrored windows and located just off U.S. 19) remarked to employees that she had spotted an extraordinary image of the Virgin Mary on the structure's south wall windows. Word got out to a local TV station, and seemingly overnight the company's parking lot swarmed with tens of thousands

Whether it was created by God or chance, the beautiful Our Lady
of Clearwater was certainly worth a double-take.

of devotees seeking a glimpse of the image.

It was certainly worth seeing. Unlike other, rather pedestrian, manifestations that have been spotted on everything from tortillas to grilled cheese sandwiches to highway underpasses, this image had a vibrant, impressionistic quality to it. Plus, it was *huge*. When the sun struck a particular bank of nine massive windows, it revealed what looked like the thirty-foot (9 m) tall outline of a woman in a hooded robe, painted in a gorgeous, iridescent rainbow of colors.

Whether it was a miracle is another question entirely. The stains that formed the shape were apparently caused by mineral deposits encrusted on the glass by the property's sprinkler system, and by oil from the palm trees that brushed against the windows. Indeed, old photos show that the Virgin Mary image on the front of the building existed for years, but it could only be clearly seen when a palm tree directly in front of it (which was exactly the same height as the apparition) was removed. The same process seems to have been at work on other parts of the building, producing, among other things, a Buddha-like outline on the east wall. The Catholic Church refused to endorse the vision. It accepted the minerals-and-palm-oil theory, labeling the image a "naturally explained phenomenon."

None of which kept an estimated half a million people from visiting it. An impromptu altar was constructed, donations were collected (and given to a local children's hospital), and souvenir stands selling T-shirts sprang up nearby. But as time passed, the image's drawing power flagged and the crowds went away. In July 1998, the Shepherds of Christ Ministries leased and then purchased the building that housed it, referring to the structure as Our Lady of Clearwater.

Unfortunately, the Lady's days are done. On March 1, 2004, the top three panes containing the Madonna wannabe's head were broken by vandals. Whatever one thinks of its origin, it was a shameful and undeserved end for a sublimely—though probably not divinely—beautiful image.

HIGHWAY TO HELL

The road to hell, it's said, is paved with good intentions. But for the better part of the twentieth century it was paved with ordinary asphalt, just like the rest of the U.S. highway system. It traversed not the infernal regions, but a huge chunk of the American Southwest, from urban centers to sun-baked desert. And according to many, its roadside attractions were—and remain—just as frightening as anything the underworld has to offer.

Route 666 was a nightmare to drive even without the flaming ghost trucks and packs of tire-shredding demon dogs.

The byway in question was called U.S. 666—the same number as the fabled "number of the beast" mentioned in Revelation 13:18. But the road didn't get its name based on arcane magical lore. It springs from a force even darker and more mysterious: the bureaucratic machina-tions of the Joint Board of Interstate Highways. Back in the 1920s, the organization assigned the designation U.S. 66 to the now-legendary Chicago-to-Los Angeles highway better known as Route 66. It was divided into five branches, with the farthest east designated U.S. 166, and the farthest west becoming U.S. 666. Of course, logically it should have been called 566, but because of a political dustup that was as dreadfully complicated as it was dreadfully boring, it wasn't.

In 1942, the road was massively extended from 141 miles (230 km) to 556 miles (900 km) by adding the twisting, mountainous Coronado Trail to its domain. In 1970, U.S. 666 reached its maximum length of 605 miles (975 km) when it was extended all the way to Monticello, Utah.

For decades, no one thought very much about the road's ill-starred numbering. It wasn't until the seventies (perhaps influenced by the *Omen* movies, which came out at about the same time) that this particular stretch of blacktop developed a reputation for being evil. Soon, every possible road specter one could imagine seemed to set up shop on its shoulders. There were tales of drivers run off the road by flame-belching trucks barreling along at one-hundred-plus miles per hour (166 km/h); packs of spectral dogs that shredded the tires of vehicles; and ghostly female hitchhikers who disappeared whenever someone was foolish enough to pull over for them.

The psychic bestiary even included a horror peculiar to the American Southwest, the magnificently named skinwalkers. These evil, shape-shifting shamans could turn themselves into anything from a crow to a wolf and made a habit of suddenly materializing in front of moving cars—or, even worse, appearing in empty backseats.

But as many a long-haul trucker knew, 666 could be a pretty hairy trip even without a sinister being riding shotgun. Immense stretches of the road knifed through searing, featureless desert. It was the sort of place where, if your car conked out, you'd see vultures long before you saw a tow truck. Other sections bobbed and weaved through treacherous mountain passes, forcing drivers to negotiate hairpin turns and steep drops that, over the years, claimed the lives of more than a few unwary motorists.

This combination of real and surreal dangers caused many drivers to simply take detours—something that didn't exactly help with economic development in the areas that U.S. 666 "served." Plus, souvenir hunters kept stealing the signs. Transportation authorities couldn't do much about the road's route, but they could do away with the demonic number, which saddled it with the nickname the Devil's Highway. In 1993, Arizona's stretch was renamed U.S. 191. In 2003, the rest became the decidedly un-satanic-sounding U.S. 491.

In their desperation, state and federal authorities succumbed to the politically correct idea that changing something's name can somehow change its nature. Unfortunately, a janitor will always be someone who cleans toilets, even if you change the title to "sanitation engineer." Likewise, in the minds of many, the Devil's Highway will always be the Devil's Highway, no matter what number you hang on it.

Get ready for one hell of a ride.

Can a simple name change evict all the ghosts and ghouls that allegedly set up shop there? No one can say. Our advice is to play it safe. If you find yourself driving a deserted stretch of U.S. 491, make sure to yield for speeding semis, ignore all hitchhikers, and keep an eye on the backseat.

THE DEVIL'S LAWN ORNAMENT

The inappropriate or excessive use of lawn statuary has caused many a neighborhood snit. That's because one man's cute little garden gnome, homey-looking concrete porch goose, or lifelike ten-point buck can be another's kitschy, property-value-destroying nightmare.

Given the discord that any one of those objects could cause if it

New Jersey boasts a bit of yard sculpture only a prince of darkness could love.

appeared suddenly in a flower bed, it's not hard to imagine the havoc wreaked when Denny Van Istendal parked his own unique bit of statuary on the lawn of his Lumberton, New Jersey, home. According to reports, his neighbors called it demonic and despicable (among a great many other things), and accused it of frightening everything from neighborhood children to the horses at a nearby stable.

One can see their point. Van Istendal's lawn ornament isn't the usual bit of crudely made, side-of-the-road goofiness. It's an eleven-foot (3.3 m) tall, three-thousand-pound (1,360 kg) statue of a Sumerian fertility god.

A really angry one, judging from the look of seething rage on its four-horned, red-eyed, skull-like head.

The statue came to Van Istendal by way of Hollywood. It was originally built as a prop for the 1955 Lana Turner movie *The Prodigal*, for which it was painted gold and equipped with light-up red eyes. There was a picture of it on the flick's poster. After its acting career (which included a couple of cameos in Tarzan movies) dried up, the piece languished for years in front of a Newark lawn service company. Then, in 1984, it was repositioned on a highway north of the Delaware town of Smyrna. First it welcomed visitors to a travel agency, then to a gallery. The piece was nicknamed the "Buddha," even though there's absolutely nothing Buddha-esque about its glowering visage.

When its former owner decided she'd had enough of the thing, Van Istendal offered $4,000 for it. Ironically, he didn't have a clue about its Hollywood origins—he just liked its looks. He hauled it to his prop-

The fertility god gets ready to move from a strip mall to Denny Van Istendal's yard. The statue doesn't seem too happy about it.

erty and carefully positioned it on a five-foot (1.5 m) mound of dirt with the setting sun at its back so that his own personal pagan god would cast an intimidating shadow across the road out front. "I think this thing overlooking my yard is kind of cool," he told the *Burlington County Times*. "If it offends you, don't look at it."

The neighborhood *was* offended and decided that no one should look at it. City officials, using an extremely free interpretation of local zoning ordinances, told Van Istendal that he had to banish his god to a spot where it couldn't be seen from the road. Van Istendal fought the ruling, stating that the statue was already concealed behind a six-foot (1.8 m) fence. Actually, "concealed" probably wasn't the right word. The "Buddha" towered over the fencing, allowing it to leer at startled motorists.

These days the statue leers at no one, save for Van Istendal and invited guests.

THE HAUNTED CAR

The four-wheeled witness to a pair of savage killings forever haunts a dark stretch of suburban road.

In Chicago, parents who want to teach their kids to be wary of strangers still tell the story of teenagers Barbara and Patricia Grimes. On December 28, 1956, the sisters went to see the Elvis Presley movie *Love Me Tender* for the eleventh time. It would be their final trip. The girls vanished without a trace. Twenty-five days later, their bodies were discovered along Devil's Creek, next to a forlorn two-lane stretch of blacktop called German Church Road.

This sort of heinous crime just didn't happen at the dawn of the baby boom. It ignited public indignation and triggered a manhunt of epic proportions. Police combed the area where the bodies were found and questioned a staggering three hundred thousand people in connection with the case. But it was all for naught. The killer of the Grimes girls got away clean. He could still, conceivably, be at large.

But perhaps not. Evidence seems to suggest that the murderer (or murderers) has passed away—and that he (or they) now endures a punishment handed down by a higher court.

The place where the girls were found is located in the southern Cook County suburb of Willow Springs. Many things about the area have changed in the last fifty years, but not everything. German Church Road is still there, and Devil's Creek still bubbles nearby. What's missing is an old ranch-style house that formerly overlooked the spot where the Grimes sisters' bodies were found—a place where the first sightings of a spectral car occurred.

The house in question was abandoned shortly after the grisly crime scene was discovered. The owners moved away so hastily that they left many of their possessions behind, including an old Buick convertible that for years sat rusting in the garage. Eventually vandals torched the place, and the ruins were leveled. A heavy chain was stretched across the entrance to the gravel driveway to keep curiosity seekers away.

Perhaps the former owners left because of the horrible events that took place so close by. Or perhaps they left because the house itself became haunted. One story associated with the spot states that, years ago, a group of teenagers visited the ruins of the old house. They jumped the driveway chain, walked up to the charred remains, and examined them under the light of the moon. But in the midst of their reverie, a dark car with no headlights came flying up the gravel road, circled the house, and disappeared.

Not surprisingly, the group decided to leave. But as they hurried down the drive to the street, they were met by police who had been alerted to the trespass by neighbors. When the kids asked if the officers saw the car, they were told that nothing had passed them. Even more telling, the chain across the driveway was still in place.

Others who have walked along German Church Road at night have reported similar encounters. A car is heard pulling onto the shoulder and idling. There's the sound of doors opening and then closing. Then the vehicle drives away. But no car is ever seen.

Much has changed along this fateful stretch of road since the fifties. The formerly lonely, tree-filled land that brackets it was turned into a housing development called Bridle Path in the late nineties. But one blast from the past remains—a dark car that, for some reason, can't leave the scene of the crime.

THE SPECTRAL HORSEMEN OF ROUTE 895

One of the quickest ways to get in and out of Richmond, Virginia, is via Route 895, a new, 8.8-mile (14 km) toll expressway also known as Pocahontas Parkway. Opened in stages between May and September 2002, it seemed to be a big hit with the commuting public. But judging from the events that followed, not everyone who lives—or, more accurately, lived—in the area was all that thrilled with it.

Toll booth attendants expect no quarter from the undead riders plaguing this Virginia expressway.

And they weren't the least bit shy about making their feelings, and their presence, known.

The strangeness began just days after the highway commenced operations. In short order, police, commuters, and toll booth staffers started seeing and hearing things. Really odd things. One of the most chilling encounters happened on the night of July 15, 2002, when a nonplussed trucker pulled into a toll plaza and told an attendant (who duly filed a report) that he'd encountered three torch-carrying, breechcloth-wearing Native Americans standing by the road. Even more unsettling, he'd also spotted two more on the road itself, directly in front of his rig. Only a quick blast from his air horn, he believed, prevented a collision.

The trucker, according to the *Richmond Times-Dispatch*, figured they might be protesters of some sort who were irked by the highway. And perhaps they were. But as the attendant he spoke to probably already knew, these particular protesters didn't seem to be human. On July 1 and 3, almost two weeks before the trucker incident, toll plaza workers themselves had called the Virginia State Police about a "trespasser" they'd seen prowling around the place—a trespasser described as having a cloudy-looking body and only the vaguest outline of a head.

The cops never found the almost-headless interloper. But soon they were busy checking out other such run-ins. An engineer working late at night to put the finishing touches on an expressway bridge reported seeing a mounted Native American warrior galloping across the span. Unaware of the recent rash of ghost sightings, he assumed the rider was merely a trespasser with a bizarre sense of fashion. The engineer tried to approach the individual and warn him to get lost, "because you're not allowed to have a horse on an interstate." But the apparition vanished before he could tell it any such thing.

The tales of ghost encounters multiplied when accounts of the strange sightings started showing up in newspapers and on TV. Motorists passing the eastbound Pocahontas Parkway toll booth reported being chased by a mounted Native American in full traditional dress. And, as if the job of night shift toll booth attendant weren't unattractive enough already, soon the employees had to endure a seemingly endless barrage of yips and energetic whoops from the nearby woods. The sounds even gave the police the creeps. "Three separate times during our watch, I heard high-pitched howls and screams," Virginia State Police spokesperson Corinne Geller told the *Times-Dispatch*. "Not the kind of screams of a person in trouble, but whooping. There were at least a dozen to fifteen [voices]. I would say every hair on my body was standing up when we heard those noises."

Not surprisingly, such tales quickly brought a rush of sightseers, would-be ghost hunters, and thrill-seeking teenagers, all of them trying to catch a glimpse of anything unusual. "Actually, the ghost is so popular, the troopers are warning ghost hunters not to get out of their cars," said Sara Cross of the Virginia Department of Transportation. "It's hazardous." Finally the throngs of people parking along 895's shoulders late at night became too large and unruly for comfort. After a brief grace period, the Virginia State Police started handing out tickets and making arrests.

But by that time, supernatural sightings had dwindled to almost nothing. Strangely, the more people who hung out at the highway, the fewer the visitations. Perhaps the ghost groupies inadvertently hit upon something that the local spirits liked even less than toll roads—crowds.

MAKING TRACKS THROUGH DEVIL'S SWAMP

If all goes as planned, workers traveling between Boston and the small bedroom communities dotting southern Massachusetts will soon have a quicker way to get to and from their city jobs. The Massachusetts Bay Transportation Authority plans to build a new railroad line that, when finished, will link Beantown with such downstate towns as Fall River and New Bedford.

If the city of Boston has its way, a new rail line could snake through one of New England's most haunted places.

But those commuters could be in for a very eventful trip. A section of the track passes through a bit of cursed ground known as the Bridgewater Triangle—a roughly two-hundred-square-mile (51,800 hectare) area that's centered on a five-thousand-acre (2,025 hectare) patch of primordial wetland known as Hockomock Swamp.

Environmentalists say it's home to many rare and wonderful creatures, including the blue-spotted salamander and the ringed boghaunter dragonfly.

All of which is well and good—and of no interest whatsoever to the average business traveler. But legend also holds that creatures far more formidable than flying bugs and slimy amphibians inhabit Hockomock—also known, tellingly, as the Devil's Swamp. The area's sodden moors form the dark heart of a paranormal hot spot that reputedly draws visitations from every sort of supernatural horror known to humanity, including (but not confined to) Bigfoot, UFOs, cattle mutilations, hauntings, and creatures so bizarre they defy description, let alone explanation.

According to local lore, the area's Native Americans were always leery of the swamp and the land surrounding it. The Europeans who displaced them soon developed an equally healthy respect—perhaps because it was said that the original inhabitants cursed the place before being driven away. This bit of real estate had its first UFO sighting back on May 10, 1760, though residents at the time referred to the phenomena, which appeared at around 10 in the morning, as a "sphere of fire." The light it radiated was so intense that it actually cast shadows. This was only a prelude of things to come. Over the last few decades, UFOs have buzzed the area on an almost weekly basis. They seem as common as the Hockomock's ringed boghaunter dragonfly.

And so, for that matter, is Bigfoot. Time and again, residents of the neighborhoods scattered throughout the Bridgewater Triangle have seen giant, hairy creatures everywhere from the woods to suburban streets. Local cops even reported that one picked up the back end of a parked (and occupied) police cruiser, then dropped it and ran away before the car's surprised occupants could react. And on more than one occasion, local police have reportedly been summoned to investigate sightings of marauding "bears," even though bears were long ago exterminated from the area. One resident in the town of Bridgewater even reported seeing a Bigfoot-like creature in her backyard casually eating a pumpkin.

As if the Bigfoot problem weren't enough, Triangle residents also must contend with regular sightings of gigantic black birds with eight- to twelve-foot (2.4–3.6 m) wingspans; a spectral dog with red eyes that in 1976 reportedly killed two ponies; and the mysterious, ritualistic slaughter of domestic animals that the authorities blame on "cultists." Floating, glowing balls of light, commonly called "spook lights," also waft about the area. And, perhaps inevitably, the locals have even sighted "black helicopters"—unmarked rotorcraft that conspiracy theorists believe are the conveyance of choice for mysterious government operatives.

The idea of running a commuter rail line through so many oddities sounds dicey at best, and downright dangerous at worst. One certainly feels for the crews who will have to install the rails straight through the UFO- and Bigfoot-infested Hockomock. Still, the folks who use the train probably shouldn't breathe a sigh of relief once they pull into the station. Consider the strange encounter that took place a few years ago, not out on the moors, but on Elm Street, which is part of a residential neighborhood in Bridgewater. There, one night a citizen reported seeing a creature furtively ducking down inside a parked car. A creature with a pale white face, no hair, no nose, no lips, and no eyebrows.

What was it? No one can say. It just proves that in the Bridgetown Triangle, weirdness can—and often does—follow you right to your front door.

PART III.

BACKYARD BEASTS

A murderous menagerie of biological anomalies, any one of which could ruin a pool party or patio barbecue

LEAPING LIZARDS

The world of the weird owes a huge debt to the picturesque town of Loveland, Ohio. This most unlikely of places has given the planet one of its most unlikely monsters.

It's hard to imagine a less-fitting setting for such a thing. Nestled against Cincinnati's northern reaches and cuddled up to the banks of the Little Miami River, this friendly municipality is a suburban Shangri La filled with antique shops, quaint restaurants, and quiet neighborhoods both new and old. It's just the sort of place that harassed urbanites dream about when they contemplate ditching their trendy but pricey downtown lofts.

But Loveland offers much more than just the strip malls and oversized chain restaurants that seem to spread like ringworm around housing-development-intensive areas. Its foremost amenity is the Loveland Bike Trail, which parallels the Little Miami. Bicyclists can enjoy a leisurely ride, buy an ice-cream cone from a sweet shop, and watch the river roll by.

Some very peculiar creatures are said to haunt the depths (and, occasionally, the banks) of the Little Miami River.

They can also, perhaps, take a moment to contemplate the race of slimy, froglike, bipedal horrors that is said to dwell in its murky depths. Abominations that, on more than one occasion, have paid their landlubber relatives unexpected visits.

The first encounter happened during May 1955, when police received a report from a man who said that, while driving home at 3:30 A.M., he spotted something "exceedingly strange."

This was definitely an understatement. The individual alleged that he spied three vaguely reptilian, vaguely froglike creatures standing by the side of the road. One held a spark-shooting wand above his head. Authorities duly investigated the scene, but no physical evidence was found. Locals chalked it up not so much to a runaway frog, but to a local loon with a runaway imagination.

And there the matter rested until March 1972, when a Loveland police officer reportedly saw something on Riverside Road at around 1:00 A.M. The cop at first thought it was a dog—but then the "dog" rose up on its hind legs to a height of three or four feet (.9 or 1.2 m). It had leathery skin, with a lizardlike or froglike face. It eyeballed the policeman for a moment, then stepped over the highway guardrail and took off for the Little Miami River down below.

The police returned to the scene several hours later but found no physical evidence except for some scrape marks on the embankment to the water. Two weeks later, another unidentified Loveland police-man reported something similar while driving down the same stretch of blacktop. Spotting what he thought was roadkill in the middle of the pavement, he got out of his cruiser to move it out of the way. But as he approached, the creature leaped to its feet and, limping as if injured, climbed over the guardrail and headed toward the river. The cop took a shot at the beast as it disappeared into the gloaming, but he apparently missed.

That same month, a farmer not far from town claimed to see another amphibian-esque entity. This was enough to help the story make the rounds of the national media. Self-appointed experts in the paranormal soon began speculating as to whether a race of intelligent frog men haunted the local rivers.

If so, they're making themselves scarce. Since 1972, there hasn't been a single encounter. Or, at least, there haven't been any publicized incidents. Perhaps the creatures have learned to keep a low profile. Or maybe they've just moved on. Giant lizard men have also been sighted in Milton, Kentucky. And in 1988 in Bishopville, South Carolina, a local reported that a seven-foot (2.1 m) tall lizardlike humanoid chased him down a country road at speeds exceeding forty miles per hour (64 km/h). So perhaps the Loveland creatures haven't just branched out to other locales. Maybe they've also decided that when dealing with humans, a good offense is the best defense.

THE BEAST OF BRAY ROAD

The town of Elkhorn, Wisconsin, located about thirty minutes south of Milwaukee, hosts a monster that's both startlingly different and heartwarmingly (well, heartwarming probably isn't the best word) traditional. According to eyewitnesses, the beast in question is huge and hairy and smelly, but it isn't Bigfoot. It's something far, far worse. Based on descriptions that go back decades, the monster that's terrified locals for years is no less than a werewolf.

Nighttime drivers should think twice about passing through the town of Elkhorn, unless they're looking for a shoulder to die on.

The phenomenon first hit the front pages on the night of October 31, 1991, when a woman named Doris Gipson was tooling down a cave-dark bit of blacktop called Bray Road. She was fooling with her car radio when the vehicle suddenly jerked, as if it had run over something. Startled, she stopped, got out, and looked under the wheels, but

A scene from the 2005 direct-to-video film *The Beast of Bray Road*.

found nothing. However, when she peered into the darkness out past the road, she was startled to see something staring back. Something that was man-sized and bipedal—and running at top speed in her direction. Terrified, Gipson jumped back into her car, fired the engine, and peeled out. The creature leaped onto her trunk as she sped away but was thrown off.

When the story hit the papers, other locals came forward to offer tales of similar encounters with an odd creature on or around that particular patch of road. Bar manager Lorianne Endrizzi reported that one night back in 1989 she'd noticed a figure lurking on the shoulder and slowed her car down for a closer look. As she cruised by she was amazed to see, within an arm's length of her car, a humanoid beast with glowing eyes, a wolflike snout, and a muscular body covered with grayish brown hair.

The news kicked up a media frenzy. Newspapers and TV outlets from around the country ran the story, and soon tourists and locals alike were cruising Bray Road at all hours looking for the creature. Not surprisingly, they didn't find it. The last of the most famous batch of sightings happened in February 1992, when a young woman named Tammy Bray (quite a coincidence) reported seeing a large, doglike creature shamble across the road in front of her car.

After that, there were no more appearances for years. Media attention faded, and news reports dried up.

But something was overlooked. The original blitz of early nineties coverage missed the fact that sightings of a strange beast in the area had been coming in sporadically for decades, and not just from the area around Bray Road. For instance, in 1936 a local night watchman named Mark Schackelman reportedly saw what he thought was a dog rooting around an old Indian burial mound nearby. But when he turned his flashlight on the creature, he saw what in later years he described as "a demon from hell"—a wolflike, man-sized monstrosity with long claws and glowing eyes.

Even more telling, communities near the Bray Road hot spot told their own stories about hairy, wolflike and apelike creatures in their midst for years. Some called it the Bluff Monster, while to others it was simply the Eddy. But whatever you want to call it, it sure gets around. In May 2004, a witness reported a beast that sounds a lot like the Bray Road horror. Only this monster was seen skulking down a residential street in Madison, Wisconsin, at around 1:00 A.M.

Not that the creature has entirely abandoned the turnpike that made it famous. It's said that in 1999 a woman who heard that a filmmaker was doing a documentary on the Bray Road beast piled her family into the car and drove out one night to try to catch him at work. They didn't see the filmmaker, but they did see his subject—a huge, hairy, bipedal canine that charged to within fifty feet (15 m) of their car, nearly scaring the life out of them.

BIG BIRDS

Nobody likes it when company drops in unannounced. Especially when it drops in out of the sky. And especially when the company in question isn't a distant relative or a next-door neighbor seeking to borrow your circular saw, but an enormous black bird with a wingspan as big as an airplane's and a taste for human flesh.

Gigantic avian predators create quite a flap when they appear out of the blue.

That's just what Lawndale, Illinois, resident Ruth Lowe had to contend with on the muggy evening of July 25, 1977. She was cleaning out the family camper in the front yard when she heard her ten-year-old son, Marlan, screaming in the backyard. Lowe, according to her own account, dashed around the house just in time to witness pretty much the last thing someone in her position would expect to witness. A gigantic black bird with an eight-foot (2.4 m) wingspan had grasped her seventy-pound (32 kg) son by the shoulders and was attempting to fly off with him.

According to Lowe, the bird came very close to succeeding. It had managed to lift the violently struggling boy off the ground and was

slowly flapping its way across the yard. But apparently the load—
and, perhaps, the number of screaming spectators it quickly attracted—
was too much to bear. The bird dropped Marlan and soared skyward,
where it flew away with a feathered companion that was every bit as
large as itself. Lowe, now joined by her husband, Jake, and their next-
door neighbors James and Betty Daniels, watched the bizarre attackers
depart. "If I had just had a can of beer earlier, then I could have said
I imagined it," James Daniels told United Press International. "But I
didn't have any beer that day."

Maybe not, but officials were quick to discredit the family's version
of events. Experts pointed out, rightly, that gigantic, child-snatching
black birds weren't exactly a common sight in the skies over Illinois,
or anywhere else in the western hemisphere, for that matter. Perhaps,
it was suggested, they might have been turkey vultures or king vultures.
But those birds, though weighing around fifty pounds (23 kg), simply
aren't big and powerful enough to contemplate picking up a struggling
boy. And since vultures prefer to dine on carrion, why would they
bother with live prey?

The consensus, at least among some people, was that the Lowes perhaps embellished the details of the encounter. And yet, to this day,
Marlan sticks by the same version of events he and his family put forth
back in 1977. They can perhaps take comfort in the fact that they're not
the only people in the area who claimed to have seen the winged behe-
moths. On the evening of July 28, a woman who was out driving not far
from Lawndale reported being buzzed by a giant bird. And a couple of
hours later on that same evening, a group of people flying model air-
planes was approached by a bird with an estimated ten-foot (3 m)
wingspan. The next day, mail carrier James Majors reported seeing two
large birds loitering over a pig farm. Suddenly one dropped out of the
sky, attacked a roughly fifty-pound (23 kg) piglet, and hauled it into the
air. Shortly thereafter it landed with its prize and was joined by its
companion. Together they dined on the catch.

If one can believe eyewitness accounts, suburban Illinois isn't the
only place to see giant airborne predators. A monster with a reported

fifteen- to twenty-foot (4.5–6 m) wingspan flew over Middletown, Ohio, in 1967. And in the seventies, there was a spate of Texas sightings, including a January 1976 encounter in which two San Benito police officers, Arturo Padillo and Homero Galvan, reportedly saw an enormous bird gliding over a canal. And Pennsylvania seems to be a hotbed for freakish flyers, with eyewitness accounts dating back to the nineteenth century.

Perhaps these were examples of an animal that Native Americans called the Thunderbird—a gigantic, supposedly mythical creature that was said to cause thunder and lightning. These days, however, it only seems to cause consternation. Though sightings continue, there's never been one made by any of the country's tens of thousands of bird-watchers. That's a bit telling, because people who can differentiate between two closely related types of finch at one hundred paces should have no trouble spotting an avian predator the size of an airliner. Also, what exactly would such giant birds eat? Maybe the cattle mutilation people should get together with the Thunderbird enthusiasts and compare notes.

BETTER LAKE THAN NEVER

Does prehistoric terror lurk in an almost-new reservoir?

It seems as if every body of water that's larger than an apartment complex retention pond comes to have a "creature" story associated with it. The most famous, of course, is the Loch Ness Monster. But there are many, many others. A beast called Champ supposedly lurks in the frigid depths of Lake Champlain. Likewise, Lake Tahoe has its Tessie and Lake Manitoba its Manipogo.

But the weirdest pedigree belongs to a Southern California monster named Hodgee. He (or she) is the supposed marine denizen of 1,234-acre (500 hectare) Lake Hodges, which serves both as a water reserve for nearby San Diego and a scenic magnet for suburban housing developments. For decades, some have claimed it is also inhabited by a primordial, dinosaur-like monster. What they haven't been able to explain is how a prehistoric animal came to live in a lake that's less than a century old. That's right, Lake Hodges is really a human-made reservoir. And a relatively new one at that.

Not surprisingly, local legend offers an explanation.

The trouble began in the early twentieth century, when it was decided that Lake Hodges—at the time a much smaller affair—could be greatly expanded by damming the river that drained it. This was begun in 1916 over the protests of the area's inhabitants, including members of the Kumeyaay Indian tribe, who said the project would disturb the water beast that lived in the river that fed the lake. The company in charge of the project, displaying all the care and concern usually shown for aboriginal rights in those days, ignored the tribe's warnings and plunged ahead, finishing work in 1918.

And then the fun started. In 1921, two companies hired to remove rocks from the new, improved lake found heavy equipment left near the shoreline knocked down and damaged. Of course, industrial espionage was suspected. But when no one owned up to the crime, some suggested that a third party—a third party with flippers and big, scary teeth—might be to blame. Suddenly the monster stories were off and running. Fishermen regularly reported strange disturbances in the water, and shoreline observers spotted dark, hard-to-make-out lumps and bumps on the surface.

According to local sources, in 1932 the Scripps Institute of Oceanography was brought in to attempt to capture Hodgee. But though the scientists employed a gigantic metal trap the size of a small house and baited with a sea lion pup, they failed to capture anything but an extremely grainy photograph taken by an underwater, tripwire-triggered camera. The original shot looks like absolutely nothing. A digitally enhanced version seems to show the very faint outline of something that resembles a wad of flattened, dried-up bubblegum. The cage work was allegedly discontinued after local uproar over the use of sea lions as bait. Incidentally, Scripps says the institute has no record of ever participating in such a project. Hoax or cover-up?

Over the decades, other sightings were reported and a handful of grainy photos of black objects lolling on the surface were taken. Then, in a truly *X-Files*-like twist, in 1956 the entire lake was intentionally poisoned, purportedly to kill off the overabundant carp population.

Some, of course, suspected that the real agenda was to do away with Hodgee once and for all.

If that was the case, then the plan failed. After the poisoning, sightings actually escalated. In 1966, a couple of families picnicking on the shore of Lake Hodges spotted and photographed a dark object that surfaced about fifty yards (45 m) offshore. Today, as more and more families come to live near the reservoir, the stories continue to trickle in. There's even a Lake Hodges Scientific Research Center dedicated to chasing the monster. Its Web site features all the Hodgee photos, along with shots of professorish men hunkered down over electronic gear.

Most locals think that the monster in their midst is either benevolent or a myth perpetrated by reservoir workers with too much time on their hands. Maybe so. But it's worth noting that though Lake Hodges is considered a great hiking and fishing spot, swimming is strictly prohibited. Maybe, as its keepers say, it's to keep the San Diego drinking water supply pristine. Or maybe, just maybe, it's to make sure Hodgee isn't tempted to go bobbing for swimmers.

HELLO KITTY

The locals swear they aren't lyin' about the giant lion terrorizing suburban Columbus, Ohio.

Just northeast of Columbus, Ohio, sits the small suburban town of Gahanna. It's not what you'd call a tourist mecca. But in the summer of 2004, it hosted an unexpected visitor that put it on front pages worldwide—and sent its terrified residents running for cover.

The visitor was reportedly a gigantic wild cat. The hysteria began on May 3, when three locals, at roughly the same time and place, reported seeing a large female lion on the loose. First, a Columbus police officer spotted an unfamiliar animal skulking along a deserted road. Shortly thereafter, a truck driver saw a large feline form crouching under a parked tractor trailer. And shortly after that, a group of railroad workers reported seeing a lionlike creature walking down some railroad tracks.

Local police immediately launched a massive search, employing heavily armed walking patrols, an infrared camera, and a helicopter to look for the creature. But they turned up nothing. More reports came in as the days wore on, but each seemed more panicky and sketchy than the last. A worker in the control tower at the local airport reported spotting a "large brown object in a field," which turned out to be a deer. Golfers found "giant paw prints" near the seventeenth hole of the Jefferson Country Club. Prints that, on closer examination, were found to be those of a big dog.

It wasn't long before the exhausted constabulary (augmented by four other agencies and the Columbus Zoo rescue unit) grew tired of crashing through the underbrush every time someone phoned in a "lion sighting." By the end of the week, the official search was suspended, and reports of big cat encounters dried up completely. Soon the only lions to be seen were the ones on souvenir T-shirts that read "I Was Eaten by the Gahanna Lion (I Got Better)." By June the entire issue was off the radar. "We're putting the lion in the cold case squad," Gahanna police lieutenant Jeff Spence told Columbus's NewsChannel 4.

So where did it go? How could so many competent people, including police officers, give detailed descriptions of what they saw, only to have it vanish into thin air? It's interesting to note that the events in Gahanna, though bizarre, are far from unique. Gigantic mystery cats are regularly sighted all over the world—especially in Great Britain, where there's a mania for them that stretches back decades. Alien big cats (ABCs for short) have been sighted all over England and Scotland. Some even get cool names, such as the Nottingham Lion and the Beast of Exmoor. Over there the tales have a distinctly Bigfoot-ish air, because there aren't any large wild felines in Europe. But in the United States, the stories often can't be dismissed out of hand, especially in mountain lion country. Those big, muscular cats are increasing their ranges nationwide, and some aren't above prowling around subdivisions at night, or picking off the occasional unwary jogger.

But that doesn't seem to be the case with the Gahanna lion. After scaring the pants off the locals, it disappeared into thin air. Or, perhaps, moved on to fresh territory. On May 13, just as things were dying down in Gahanna, an elementary school in the nearby town of Kirkersville suspended recess after a catlike creature was spotted prowling the perimeter of the school grounds. One witness said it "kind of walked like a lion." And on July 10, the Associated Press reported that Madison Township firefighter Ed Dildin spotted a lionlike animal crossing a cornfield near the town of Canal Winchester, thirteen miles (21 km) to the southeast of Gahanna.

So maybe the creature hasn't vanished after all. Maybe it's just looking for better hunting.

THE DOVER DEMON

For going on three decades, the inhabitants of the upscale Beantown suburb of Dover have wondered what manner of man, beast, or spirit paid a brief but memorable visit to their town in the spring of 1977. The mystery began on the night of April 21, when seventeen-year-old Bill Bartlett was driving two friends home at around ten in the evening. As his Volkswagen puttered down Farm Street, Bartlett saw what he thought was some sort of animal climbing over a stone wall on the road's left side. But when he got close enough for his headlights to illuminate it, he spied what looked like a spindly stick figure with an egg-shaped head and peach-colored skin. As the VW passed at around 40 miles per hour (64 km/h) the creature turned and stared at him with

What has a puny body, a giant head, orange eyes, and long, spindly legs? That's what the residents of one suburban Boston town would like to know.

glowing orange eyes—the only features on an otherwise featureless face.

Understandably, Bartlett elected not to stop and investigate. Instead, he continued down the road for a short distance, then pulled over and told his two friends—who had missed the whole thing—what he had seen. About fifteen minutes later, after considerable debate, they screwed up their courage and returned to the scene of the sighting. But by that time there was nothing more to witness.

Nonplussed, Bartlett dropped his friends off at their homes and then returned to his own house, where he drew a crude-looking picture of what he had seen.

Only a couple of hours later, fifteen-year-old John Baxter encountered a similar entity shortly after walking his girlfriend to her Miller Hill Road home in Dover. Only his was a far more intimate and lengthy confrontation, because he was on foot at the time. As he approached the intersection of Miller Hill Road and Farm Street, he noticed another pedestrian off in the distance, coming his way. Baxter called to the figure, believing it was someone he knew—or, at the very least, believing it was a fellow human being.

He soon realized he was mistaken on both counts. As he continued to close the distance to the lone figure, he saw that the "person" was both impossibly short and endowed with an impossibly huge head. Finally, with only about twenty paces separating them, the two stopped walking and regarded each other uncertainly.

Incredibly, the creature's nerves failed first. When Baxter asked who it was and took one more tentative step forward, the entity bolted for the woods, disappearing into the underbrush. The kid pursued, finally catching up with his quarry on the edge of a small brook. The thing was standing stock-still, clutching rocks along the rubble-strewn banks with its exceptionally long fingers and toes.

And it was staring at him.

Only then did Baxter get his first good look at the creature, with its giant head, featureless face, and big, glowing eyes. Not surprisingly, he quickly reevaluated the wisdom of pursuing such an odd beast without any sort of backup, even though it was no bigger than a first-grader.

The kid cleared out as fast as he could, walked back to the road, and flagged down a ride that took him home. Once there, he too drew a picture of the thing he'd encountered.

But the visitation wasn't quite over. Around midnight on the very next night, fifteen-year-old Abby Brabham was getting a ride home from her boyfriend, Will Taintor. As they headed west on Springdale Avenue, both noticed a strange creature with a tiny body and a big head. "It had bright green eyes and the eyes were just glowing, like they were just looking exactly at me," Brabham told authorities later.

At that point, if a thousand teens-meet-monsters movies are to be believed, the kids would have stopped their car and piled out to investigate. But in a testament to the common sense and survival skills of Dover's youth, they did nothing of the sort. Just seconds after the encounter, Taintor asked his girlfriend if she'd seen what he'd seen. "Yeah," she reportedly responded. "Lock the doors, let's get out of here. Hurry up."

The incidents received the usual, lightning-quick blast of national publicity. Bartlett and Baxter's startlingly similar drawings of the demon were plastered on supermarket tabloids across the globe. Then the entire subject faded into obscurity. Theories about what the kids saw ran the gamut from a space alien to a stupendously misidentified young moose. About the only thing that's known with certainty is that the Dover Demon hasn't returned—and that Taintor and his distinctly uncurious girlfriend made the right call by staying in the car.

ATTACK OF THE KILLER SPORES

These days, stories of mold-infested houses are old news. An entire industry has sprung up to rid afflicted domiciles of this fuzzy horror, which seems to gain a foothold in damp basements, inside walls, and anywhere else moisture accumulates. But those infestations are mere inconveniences compared to one of the very first—and very worst—of all mold invasions. It happened in the tiny town of Elkin, North Carolina, where a horrified couple fought a battle royal against ravenous spore spawn bent on taking over their property.

And this time, the mold won.

The nightmare began in the summer of 1961, when Mr. and Mrs. Grady Norman laid down linoleum flooring in two rooms of their house. Shortly thereafter, they both developed asthmalike respiratory troubles—troubles that got worse whenever they visited the refurbished spaces. Perplexed, they finally pulled up a corner of the

You may not like this microscopic home invader at first, but after a while it starts to grow on you.

linoleum to see what it might hide. What they found was a lush layer of gray-green mold.

The Normans immediately ripped out the flooring, exposing a veritable lawn of velvety growth. The couple doused the floors with powerful cleansers, scrubbed away every trace of the matted mess, and then shellacked the floors. But within two days the mold came back, this time infesting walls, furniture, clothing, and anything else that held still long enough for it to colonize. Trying to clean the mess was torture, because disturbing the mold kicked up clouds of dust that burned their skin and triggered violent coughing fits. Finally the local health department stepped in. After warning that the house was far too dangerous to inhabit, authorities discovered that only a carbolic acid solution seemed to hinder the mold's growth. Unfortunately, this highly caustic "cure" caused almost as much damage as the infestation.

Finally, after months of fighting a losing battle against the gray-green invader, the Norman family gave up and moved away. Incredibly, the next year someone actually bought their old house and tried to clean it up. Apparently he had about as much luck as the previous inhabitants, because he quickly threw in the towel and left the property vacant. It stood empty for almost three decades until it was bulldozed in 1989.

The mold apparently didn't follow the Normans to their new address—though some believe that years later they were still feeling its wrath. The couple's daughter, who spoke later to Maryland-based researcher Michael A. Frizzell, recalled that at the height of the invasion, health authorities identified the velvety intruder as a combination of penicillin and aspergillus molds. While penicillin in its myriad forms is usually benign, aspergillus can cause infections, lung disease, even cancer.

Which might explain why, as their daughter recalls, the elder Normans both developed emphysema several years after their epic battle. Maybe it wasn't just happenstance. Maybe it was one last parting insult from the unstoppable spores.

THE TERROR OF LEVITTOWN

America's first suburbs are overrun with UFOs, ghosts, and Bigfoot. Yes, Bigfoot.

It's safe to say that America's cookie-cutter subdivisions probably wouldn't exist without the Levitt brothers, Alfred and William. After World War II, they became home-building gurus, applying mass production principles to housing construction. Their goal, so amply realized in Levittown, New York, was to create relatively cheap, good-quality housing for America's working stiffs, and to do it tout de suite. In 1947, Levittown, New York, was opened. Soon it grew (social critics might say metastasized) to include more than seventeen thousand homes.

This scratch-made city, with its droning sameness and bourgeois pretensions, became a lightning rod for critics of suburban sprawl. And as one might expect, soon the town began to manifest the very social ills its designers hoped to leave behind—everything from crime and drugs to rampant UFO sightings and spectral black dogs.

For whatever reason, Levittown really packs in the space aliens.

The numerous sightings include a "baton-shaped UFO" spotted by a group of residents on the evening of October 2, 1999. "This thing was huge," one witness told the World Wide UFO Reporting Center. "It looked like a giant baton with a dimly lit sphere on each end. I watched it for at least five seconds as it headed from east to west." Another witness reported seeing a glowing, oval-shaped craft that hung motionless in the sky for about two minutes before scooting off into the unknown. And on January 29, 2004, two witnesses reported being buzzed by a pair of triangular objects with bright lights on their undersides.

Perhaps the UFOs are interested in the area's ghosts. One of the best local legends concerns a house with a green-shingled roof on Appletree Drive. Back in the 1950s, it was owned by a very old woman with a very large black dog. The woman was eventually evicted from the house and wound up living out of her car, in which she was found dead a couple of years later. Her giant dog still haunts its old Appletree Drive address, tromping up and down the stairs and staring with glowing red eyes at occupants of the bedroom at the top right of the stairs. Underneath those stairs the woman herself, wearing a long black dress, occasionally puts in an appearance.

Thankfully, residents of the *other* Levittown—the one located in Bucks County, Pennsylvania—have so far encountered no such problems. Their own sprawling, preplanned community, which was also built by the Levitt brothers, remains more or less free of ghosts and aliens. Their main beef is with Bigfoot.

This may come as a surprise to those who associate the presence of giant, hairy hominids with the Himalayas or, at the very least, the wilds of the Pacific Northwest. But as the members of the Pennsylvania Bigfoot Society are happy to explain (often at great length), the Quaker State is absolutely crawling with man-apes. Reports have placed them in practically every county, doing everything from swimming in Lake Erie to peeking in the windows of private residences. But one of the more interesting manifestations happened in December 2004, when self-described Bigfoot hunter Stuart Caesar took pictures of a set of tracks his girlfriend discovered near Levittown, Pennsylvania's, Magnolia Hill section. Caesar followed the sixteen-inch (40 cm) prints for about half a mile (800 m) before the trail petered out beside a creek. "There were toe markings . . . the tracks were smooth, indicating a heel and ball of a foot," he told the *Bucks County Courier Times*.

Is Bigfoot a better neighbor than UFOs and ghosts? Maybe so. Granted, spotting an eight-foot (2.4 m) tall ape lumbering across one's backyard would be no picnic, but at least they've never been known to steal people's souls or kidnap them for bizarre medical experiments. So far, at least.

THE GOATMAN COMETH

Is it appropriate to feel pity for an abomination? If so, then Maryland's legendary Goatman probably deserves some. Ever since his reported birth in a government laboratory several decades ago, he's fought an uphill battle to gain street cred and respect. Because let's face it: His name isn't exactly synonymous with terror. The mere mention of Bigfoot, gray-skinned aliens, or even a run-of-the-mill ghost can send chills down the spines of the timid. But Goatman? Not so much.

The suburban streets and parks of Maryland are haunted by a highly original—if somewhat lame—beast.

For decades, Maryland (specifically, the suburbs around Washington, D.C.) has been stalked by a creature variously described as having a goat's head and a man's body, or a goat's hindquarters and a man's trunk and face. But either way, the image doesn't exactly evoke visceral terror. Far from it. The Goatman is so far from scary that a version of the entity (called Goat Boy) was turned into a recurring *Saturday Night Live* character.

The backstory developed to explain this biological anomaly is just as entertaining—and far more inventive—than the *SNL* sketch. According to information unearthed primarily by Maryland high school kids, this monstrosity is the product of a hideously misguided attempt to combine goat and human DNA that was carried out at the United States Agricultural Research Center in Beltsville, Maryland. Given the loathsome final product, one wonders if the "experiment" that produced it involved wine, candles, and a close encounter with one very special goat.

However it was accomplished, it's doubtful this particular scientific endeavor will ever be written up in a peer-reviewed journal.

The person least satisfied with the experiment's results seems to be Goatman. Appalled by his appearance and furious at the human race, he haunts the communities surrounding the nation's capital, killing and eating pets and terrifying (or, perhaps, mildly startling) any humans he encounters. Some versions of the story maintain that Goatman also carries an ax. This might come in handy for dismembering prey. Goats may be good at gnawing on tin cans, but they're famously ineffective at lacerating flesh.

The beast's favorite activities include breaking into houses and tussling with the occupants, surprising trysting teenagers as they make out in their cars beside lonely roads, and, perhaps most famously, killing and partially consuming pets. One of the biggest blowups happened in the fall of 1971, when the *Prince George's County News*, on what must have been an excruciatingly slow news day, ran a front-page story about the discovery of the body of a mutilated dog. Its owners said the animal had disappeared from their yard sometime on the night of November 3, shortly before they glimpsed some sort of hulking creature lurking in the dark.

The story had several repercussions. It turned the Goatman into a statewide phenomenon, and it transformed the road where the dog-napping incident allegedly happened into the necking spot *par excel-*

lence for local teens.

Today the not-very-scary Goatman of Maryland has received the ultimate form of flattery—imitation. Versions of the creature are now said to inhabit pretty much every state in America. A seven-foot (2.1 m) tall rendition haunts Alabama, and in eastern Texas one was spotted by hunters in 1972. In California there are even stories of "Chevo" (the Spanish word for goat) Man.

Not that he still isn't seen in the state that gave him his start. In August 2000, a construction crew allegedly spotted a hairy, twelve-foot (3.6 m) tall biped lumbering through a D.C. suburb. Newspaper accounts spun it as a Bigfoot sighting, but the locals knew better. This was Goatman's work.

PART

REALLY DESPERATE HOUSEWIVES

Suburban sirens who turned to violence
because their men did them wrong—or
because they were evil, or crazy, or both

DEATH BECOMES HIM

Movies and TV crime shows make disposing of a dead body seem relatively easy. One simply tosses it into the expansive, tarp-lined trunk of an American-made luxury sedan (big Lincolns are ideal), trundles the whole mess out to an empty field, and digs a hole. But sometimes death doesn't imitate art. Suppose you don't have a big, American-made luxury sedan? Or what if you killed someone in the heat of the moment and didn't have time to

Sometimes a corpse can be hidden in plain sight. Just make sure you have plenty of air freshener.

hatch a foolproof disposal scheme? Or, worst of all, suppose you're a brand-new (self-made) widow with toddlers at your feet, living in a small town where everyone knows everyone else's business. Where do you take the body then?

Well, if you're Dixie Shanahan of Defiance, Iowa, you don't take it anywhere. In the most literal (and gruesome) sense, you simply live with what you've done. No matter how much it stinks.

Dixie's life wasn't exactly a bed of roses anyway. The longtime resident of Defiance, located to the north of Des Moines, had spent almost two decades with her husband, Scott Shanahan. By all accounts, Scott was quite a piece of work. Moody and violent, he regularly beat Dixie to within an inch of her life. It was an open secret around town, though no one said or did much about it. Nevertheless, when Dixie wore long sleeves in the middle of summer and sunglasses indoors and on cloudy days, people figured they knew why.

Over the years, Scott got hauled in by the cops a few times for assault. Dixie also tried to leave him on several occasions, only to return. Her reason, she said later, was that she wanted her two kids to have a father. Trouble was, their father didn't seem all that interested in having kids. Dixie asserted that when Scott found out she was pregnant for a third time, he went ballistic, savagely beating her for several days. Finally, as she lay on the floor, he loaded a shotgun, pointed it

Dixie Shanahan, no pro at covering up a killing, gets taken away.

at her, and allegedly said, "This day isn't over yet. I will kill you."

At this point the chain of events gets murky, to say the least. If Dixie is to be believed, Scott then gathered all the phones in the house and retreated to the couple's bedroom . . . for a nap. After an interlude, Dixie supposedly went after him, to get a phone. There was a confrontation, and she killed him with a blast from the shotgun. Or perhaps there wasn't a confrontation. Forensics experts say Scott was shot in the back of the head while he was lying on the bed in the fetal position with a pillow tucked between his knees. Not exactly an attack posture.

Whatever the exact order of events, the final result was the same. Scott wound up with his brains fanned all over the mattress. And Dixie, faced with dealing with the mess, elected to do nothing. She simply opened the tiny bedroom's rear window for ventilation, locked the murder scene up tight, and never set foot inside it again. She did, however, stuff a towel under the door to staunch the olfactory unpleasantness and put scented room fresheners in the hallway outside.

Things must have gotten thick very quickly, because the killing took place in August 2002. But in spite of the fact that there must have been one very incriminating smell issuing from the back of the Shanahan household, everyone accepted Dixie's explanation that Scott had simply run off and left her. Without taking his car. Or his truck. Or his dog. Or a stitch of clothes.

Fortunately for her, the folks in Defiance didn't seem to give a damn about where Scott had gotten to, so long as he stayed there. Even his family wasn't exactly worried sick. "No one cared that he wasn't around," one of his relatives blithely told the *Des Moines Register*. "He was evil."

During the fourteen months Scott lay decomposing in the master bedroom, the lives of Dixie and her kids started taking off. She had previously been a nurse's aide, until her control freak husband forced her to quit working and stay home. Having removed that particular career hurdle, Dixie started taking online classes with an eye toward getting a job. Likewise, the kids began improving in school.

Her only mistake (besides leaving the body in the bedroom, of course) was to unceremoniously toss out Scott's clothes, and to sell both his work tools and his prized 1967 Chevy. Such eye-catching brazenness finally prompted someone, somewhere, to call the local sheriff's department in July 2003. The Good Samaritan pointed out that Scott Shanahan was still missing—and that his wife didn't seem to think he was coming back.

The authorities investigated the disappearance for weeks, in the process turning up tantalizing tidbits of information. Most tellingly, they learned that Dixie had been forging her husband's name on personal checks. Finally, in October 2003, the police gained access to the Shanahan home. In short order, in the bedroom that the couple had once shared, they found both the murder weapon and the murder victim, the latter much the worse for wear.

After Dixie's arrest, Defiance residents held bake sales and took up collections to help her make her $15,000 bail. But there wasn't much the locals could do about her day in court. During the trial much was made of the fact that Scott was done in by a shotgun blast to the back

Scott Shanahan

of the head—not the sort of injury usually received by someone making a frontal assault. It was the defense's assertion that Dixie shot her husband not in the heat of conflict, but as he slept.

In the end, she was found innocent of first-degree murder but guilty of second-degree murder, which carries a mandatory thirty-five-year minimum sentence. Though Dixie optimistically remarried a month before the start of her trial, she won't even get a parole hearing until she's seventy-one years old.

The residents of Defiance bemoaned her fate and started a campaign to convince the governor to reduce her sentence. Too bad no one thought to intervene when she was being beaten black-and-blue, or the entire mess could have been avoided.

THE SOCCER MOM'S SECRET

This "model" citizen concealed enough scary secrets to fill a minivan.

If soccer moms had a sorority, Melinda Raisch could have been chapter president. She raised three kids in Columbus, Ohio's, upscale suburban enclave of Delaware County, where she lived with her husband, a successful dentist to whom she'd been married for many years. She also kept busy in community organizations ranging from her church to the PTA.

She was, by any measure, a model citizen. That's why it seemed so peculiar when, in 2001, detectives from the small town of Olathe, Kansas, paid a visit to her family's large brick home. They wanted to reminisce with her about the old days. Back when she was Melinda Harmon, the young wife of a junior bank executive named David Harmon—a man who, in 1982, was bludgeoned to death by housebreakers as the couple lay in bed. Or at least that was what Melinda told authorities. She claimed she'd been right there beside him, yet she somehow escaped with barely a scratch. And the "housebreakers" on whom she blamed the attack were never found. No wonder the cops couldn't get the case out of their minds, even after so many years. "It's always been sort of an open wound to a lot of people for a long time," Johnson County district attorney Paul Morrison told the *Olathe News*. "An open wound for the whole community."

Thanks to the men from Olathe, Melinda Raisch's neighbors would soon learn that the woman they thought they knew had lived an entirely different life before coming to Ohio. One that she'd gone to great pains to put behind her. One that included murder.

Melinda Raisch went from Midwestern soccer mom to convicted killer—all because she couldn't stick to her story.

Alleged accomplice Mark Mangelsdorf gets grilled.

The story began in 1973, when Melinda, then known by her maiden name of Lambert, met her husband-to-be, David Harmon, at an Ithaca, New York, youth camp. The two were deeply religious. After marrying in 1977, they moved to tiny Olathe, home of MidAmerica Nazarene University. Theirs seemed to be a happy, almost ideal, union. Melinda got a job in the dean's office, and David worked at the Patrons State Bank & Trust, located on the town square.

All of which made his death, and what came afterward, so terribly unsettling. On the night of February 28, 1982, Melinda called the police and reported that two men had burst into the couple's bedroom and attacked them. She said they wanted the keys to the bank, and when she surrendered them they knocked her unconscious. She'd awakened about an hour later, fled to her neighbor's home, and called for help.

When the cops arrived, they found a crime scene that was both peculiarly violent and, in some ways, just plain peculiar. David had been so savagely beaten that his blood covered the walls and ceiling and his face was unidentifiable. Yet Melinda bore only a couple of superficial bruises. Plus, she seemed less concerned about her husband's death than she was about contacting (even before her parents) a MidAmerica Nazarene student named Mark Mangelsdorf, whom she had met through her job at the dean's office.

Mangelsdorf was a big man on campus—a charismatic, good-looking guy only a few years younger than the Harmons. Melinda had introduced him to David, and they had become, by all accounts, fast friends. In fact, the two men were regular racquetball partners. They played a match on the very morning of the murder.

As soon as he heard about the killing, Mangelsdorf went to the Harmon house. Police couldn't help but notice that, even though it was the middle of the night, his hair was freshly washed. Also, they were troubled by the story Melinda gave. Why would two killers beat her husband so brutally, but not her? And if they wanted the keys to the bank so badly, why was there never a subsequent robbery?

But that wasn't the most intriguing thing that happened during the investigation's opening hours. When police used a tracking dog to try to catch the perpetrators' scent, it followed its nose straight to the Dumpster outside Mangelsdorf's residence. But a search through the trash—and a careful probe of a nearby dump—turned up nothing.

In the ensuing days, police extensively grilled both Mangelsdorf and Melinda. Arrests seemed imminent. But both continued to profess innocence, and no hard physical evidence turned up to prove otherwise. Slowly, the case went cold. Within days of the killing, Melinda blew town to rejoin her family in Ohio. Mangelsdorf stayed and graduated from college that year, receiving a standing ovation from his classmates. But just like Melinda, once he left Olathe he never came back.

And there matters stood until 2001, when detectives asked the woman now known as Melinda Raisch if they could talk to her again about the long-ago incident. During the encounter they hinted that new DNA evidence—evidence impossible to extract at the time of the killing—had come to light. In fact, the cops had nothing of the sort. But they hoped that the idea of a bunch of CSI types taking a crack at the case might rattle Melinda's cage.

And it did. In a videotaped statement, she intimated for the first time that her relationship with Mangelsdorf might have strayed into impropriety. And that, just perhaps, they'd discussed what it would be like if he were her husband instead of David. Even more damning, she was caught on tape telling the police that on the night of the murder there might have been just one assailant, and that, "in my heart I knew it was Mangelsdorf."

Melinda's decision to tinker with a story that served her for decades—and to try to pin everything on Mangelsdorf—proved her undoing. Oiled with a brand-new version of that deadly night's events, the wheels of justice started turning again. Melinda was arrested—as was Mangelsdorf, who had become a wealthy business executive and father of four and lived in upstate New York.

During the soccer mom's trial, all sorts of interesting tidbits came to light. On the day of the murder, Mangelsdorf spent a great deal of time at the Harmon household with Melinda, unchaperoned. On the stand she said they "took naps" and went for a walk. But others cast their relationship in a less platonic light. A university employee who shared office space with Melinda actually lectured her about the flirting she saw between Melinda and Mangelsdorf. She clucked that having a relationship with a student was a "dangerous situation."

Even more damning, forensics experts testified that the crime scene had been tinkered with before the cops arrived. Among other things, David's body was repositioned, and the shower curtain in the bathroom tested positive for blood. It certainly looked as if someone had washed up after the crime.

The evidence was enough, finally, to convince a jury that Melinda Raisch, aka Melinda Harmon, was guilty of murder and conspiracy to commit murder, for which she got fifteen years to life. While the soccer mom cools her heels in prison, Mangelsdorf—who had also transformed himself into the very model of suburban propriety—awaits his turn in a Kansas courtroom.

SERIAL MOM

If Sharon Kinne had played her cards right, she could have become a feminist icon. In 1960, this twenty-year-old Jackson County, Missouri, housewife and mother of two was living a life of quiet desperation, trapped in a loveless marriage and yearning to break free. Finally she found the courage to escape her bourgeois surroundings, develop her hidden talents, and pursue a career in a field formerly thought to be the sole preserve of men.

When her hubby refused to buy her a sports car, this put~upon housewife pulled a gun.

And yet you're far more likely to find her on the cover of *True Crime* than *Ms.* Why? Because Kinne's talent was for murder. And her "career" was that of mad dog killer.

Her transformation from domestic goddess to black widow began when she and her husband, James, got into a long-running argument about her desire to buy a new Thunderbird. She couldn't make a very strong case for the purchase, however, because as she well knew, they were deeply in debt. Kinne even exacerbated the problem by lying about paying the bills. Also, she was having an affair with an old high school buddy, John Boldizs.

It's not surprising that James not only nixed the Thunderbird deal, but on March 19, 1960, told his wife that he wanted a divorce. This vexed Kinne greatly. So she waited until her husband lay down on the couch to take a nap, shot him in the head with a .22-caliber pistol, then blamed the entire thing on her two-year-old daughter, Dana, whom she said was playing with the weapon when it went off.

Incredibly, the cops bought her story. Kinne collected her husband's life insurance money and immediately used it to buy a T-bird. She also started an affair with the guy who sold it to her, Walter Jones. By May (about two months after she'd killed her hubby), she announced that she was pregnant by Jones and that he should marry her.

Unfortunately for Kinne, her boyfriend already had a wife—a woman named Patricia Jones. But not for long. When Patricia suddenly vanished, Kinne told Walter that she and Patricia had met and that she'd told his wife he was having an affair with her sister (Kinne didn't even have a sister). Perhaps Patricia had run off, Kinne suggested. But Walter, well aware of his girlfriend's track record, didn't buy it. He put a knife to her throat and threatened her life if she didn't come clean. Kinne agreed to "look for" Patricia—and wouldn't you know it, she and her other boyfriend, John Boldizs, managed to locate the woman's bullet-ridden corpse, dumped at a local lover's lane.

That was enough for the cops, especially after they found out Patricia was murdered by the same caliber and type of weapon that had offed James. Kinne was charged with killing both of them. She was found innocent in the Patricia Jones case, but was convicted of murdering her husband. She was sentenced to life imprisonment, but within a year the conviction was overturned. A second and then a third trial was ordered, but both ended in mistrials. A fourth was planned for October 1964, but before it convened Kinne skipped town for Mexico with a small-time hood named Samuel Puglise.

This would have been the ideal moment to fade into the scenery. But that's a tough thing to do when you can't stop killing people.

Sharon "La Pistolera" Kinne cools her heels—briefly—behind bars.

Shortly after the couple arrived in Mexico, Kinne ditched her "boyfriend" at his hotel and hooked up with Francisco Parades Ordonoz. The two checked in at another hotel, where they registered as husband and wife. And then, not long afterward, Kinne shot Ordonoz twice in the heart, killing him. She tried to make her escape, but the hotel manager refused to unlock the building's gated entrance and let her drive away. Not surprisingly, Kinne elected to shoot him. But this time she only injured her victim. He managed to hold her until police arrived.

Kinne was arrested by the Mexican cops, tried, and sentenced to ten years in prison. She appealed, and for her trouble her jail time was actually increased to thirteen years. Not that she would serve it. On December 7, 1969, she somehow managed to escape from the women's prison in Iztapalapa. She hasn't been seen since. No doubt she's still out there somewhere, a crotchety old lady in her late sixties with a lot of things to hide. If you run into her, try not to make her mad. Her fellow inmates didn't call her La Pistolera for nothing.

LOVE AND BULLETS

Divorce can be an ugly thing. But you'd be hard-pressed to find an uglier divorce than the drawn-out, humiliating, bombastic marital dissolution of Dan and Betty Broderick. The years-long ordeal was like a bad soap opera— a bad soap opera with an ending directed by Quentin Tarantino.

Things started out promising enough. In fact, the couple's union seemed like the American dream. The Brodericks

Beware the fury of a woman scorned. Especially if that woman packs a pistol and isn't afraid to use it.

married on April 12, 1969. Betty bore four children: two boys and two girls. She also worked to help put Dan through both medical and law school so that he could become a medical malpractice attorney. Finally, after hubby gathered up all the necessary degrees, he got a job with the San Diego law firm of Gray, Cary, Ames, and Fry. In 1978, Dan started his own practice and was soon pulling in well over $1 million a year. The whole clan moved into an expensive La Jolla home. But then, at a 1983 party, hubby spotted a twenty-one-year-old former flight attendant turned law firm receptionist named Linda Kolkena. Betty, who was on his arm at the time of this fateful first encounter, heard her husband whisper to a chum, "Isn't she beautiful?"

Shortly thereafter, Dan hired Linda as his personal assistant. Even though she supposedly couldn't type.

It didn't take long for Betty to figure out exactly what Linda was assisting her husband with. In the summer of 1983, while the couple was vacationing in New York, she caught him in the hotel lobby having an intimate conversation with Linda. And later, on a family trip to England, Betty learned he'd sent flowers to his "assistant."

The big showdown happened on Dan's thirty-ninth birthday. Betty, who was in counseling to deal with her "unreasonable" fears that her husband was cheating on her, showed up unannounced at his office with roses and a bottle of champagne. All she discovered was evidence of a small party, and the fact that her husband and his assistant were both gone. No one could say where, but she assumed, correctly, that Linda was reviewing her husband's briefs.

That was all Betty needed. She immediately marched home, gathered up all of Dan's expensive suits, piled them up in the backyard, doused them in gasoline, and tossed a match.

Incredibly, Dan continued to deny the affair until February 1984, when he finally came clean to Betty. Not to apologize, but to explain why he was filing for a legal separation. The family had recently moved out of their home and into a rental house while some renovations were done. Dan, without further ado, ditched his wife and kids at the rental and returned to the big house in La Jolla. The affair with Linda became public knowledge. Not long after, Betty was served with divorce papers.

It was all downhill—way downhill—from there. The big-time attorney left his family high and dry, giving them small amounts of money whenever the spirit moved him. His behavior would have tried the patience of a saint.

But Betty was no saint. As things got tougher, she became more emotionally unstable. Once, she stopped in at the La Jolla house to see the

Put-upon divorcée-turned-murderer Betty Broderick breaks down on the stand.

kids and found a homemade Boston cream pie in the kitchen. She took it upstairs and smeared it all over the bed and on Dan's now-replenished wardrobe. Dan responded by slapping a restraining order on her, which she violated a couple of days later by slinging a wine bottle through one of the home's windows.

Things weren't going any better on the legal front. Dan cast such a long shadow over the San Diego court system that Betty had to go all the way to Los Angeles to find an attorney to represent her. One of the biggest challenges he faced was getting his client to quit violating the restraining order and verbally harassing Dan at every opportunity. On Christmas Day, 1985, while Dan and Linda were away on vacation with the kids, Betty broke into the La Jolla house and, among other things, destroyed every present under the tree marked "To Linda."

Dan counterattacked by selling the house, which by a legal maneuver he was able to accomplish without his wife's consent. Then he bought a new place for himself and Linda—a columned mansion in an old-money part of San Diego called Balboa Park. Betty retaliated by driving her minivan straight through the home's front door. This earned her a brief stint in a mental hospital. Afterward, she made a habit of leaving obscene diatribes on Dan's phone.

Finally, in January 1989, an eight-day closed trial put the legal seal on the divorce. Betty, for some utterly unfathomable reason, chose to represent herself. And Dan took her to the cleaners. In addition to getting custody of the three kids still under age eighteen, he was ordered to pay the woman who put him through medical and law school less than $30,000 in cash. Betty wound up living in an apartment across the street from a strip mall. Dan and Linda, on the other hand, got married.

Finally, on November 5 of that same year, Betty snapped. She packed a .38-caliber pistol into her purse and went to pay Dan and Linda a social call. Using a key she'd stolen from one of her daughters, she entered the house and padded upstairs to the bedroom where the couple slept. Linda got two quick slugs in the chest. Dan, roused by the shots that killed his new wife, was also dispatched. And then Betty, her work done, turned herself in to the cops.

There followed a long, headline-grabbing trial, at which all the events surrounding the divorce and the double murder were laid out. Perhaps not surprisingly, it produced a hung jury. One panel member supposedly told the press that, after hearing how Dan had acted, he'd wondered, "What took her so long?"

A second trial was convened in October 1991. This time Betty was found guilty of two counts of second-degree murder. Today she resides at the Central California Women's Facility at Chowchilla. She's eligible for parole in 2011. As she wiles away the years in the stir, perhaps she can take solace in her status as a poster girl for put-upon women everywhere. After all, they even made a Lifetime TV movie about her.

REST IN PIECES

In the shadow of Boston sits the town of Somerville, Massachusetts, a little community that, until recently, harbored a very strange secret. It was in the keeping of Geraldine "Geri" E. Kelley, a California transplant who passed away November 12, 2004, at the age of fifty-four. On her deathbed she offered an unexpected confession that stunned not only her family, but the community at large.

A Boston-area widow kept her friends close and the corpse of her late husband closer.

Geri had always claimed that her husband, John, had been killed years earlier in a Las Vegas traffic accident. But this wasn't the whole truth. Actually, it wasn't the truth at all. Her husband wasn't done in by a car, but by a couple of bullets to the brain, courtesy of Geri's own gun. Incredibly, that wasn't the worst of it. Geri had told everyone that he was buried someplace out West. But John T. Kelly wasn't resting in peace in a grave half a continent away. He was right there in Somerville, stashed in a storage locker, resting in pieces.

Specifically, he was in a bin Geri rented at a facility called Planet

Self Storage. The police, when informed of her claims, paid the place a quick visit. There, in a musty, rank-smelling room, they found John. Or rather, all that remained of him after spending the last of the twentieth century and the first years of the twenty-first inside two plastic garbage bags stuffed in a six-by-three-foot (1.8 x .9 m) freezer, which had been locked and taped shut.

Apparently, police surmise, he came to this unhappy state of affairs back in 1991. Geri and John were live-in comanagers at the Victoria Motel in Ventura, California. The couple got in loud, regular fights, and Geri would tell anyone who cared to listen that John was an abusive drunk. Finally, she must have snapped. Staffers recall that one night she called and asked for someone to cover for her at the hotel because her husband had been in a bad accident.

And that was the last anyone ever saw of John.

Anyone save for Geri, who must have spent a considerable amount of time bagging, taping, and (because he did, after all, wind up in two bags) chopping. No one knows where she kept the body while in

John Kelley, all in one piece.

Planet Self Storage, John Kelley's almost-final resting place.

California, but a year after she moved to Somerville in 1997, she shipped the trussed-up freezer to Planet Self Storage, where it languished until police found it. "It's not every day that they find a dead body in one of my storage facilities," Bryce Grefe, the facility's owner, told the *Boston Globe*. "It just doesn't happen on a regular basis."

What truly boggles the mind is how, in this age of forensics experts and DNA evidence, Geri got away with it. Indeed, that old freezer would probably still be sitting in a dank corner somewhere had its owner not ratted herself out. It's not as if she had a fantastic alibi—or any alibi at all. To explain her husband's disappearance, she fibbed about a Vegas car accident. This humongous whopper could have been blown apart with a couple of quick calls to Sin City hospitals. But it seems no one ever bothered to make those calls. Not even the couple's daughter, who over the years became estranged from her mother because she refused to say where her father's grave could be found. Reportedly she told her child, "Nobody needs to know."

Which leads to the biggest mystery of all. Why didn't Geri just dump the body somewhere, rather than keep it around for years and then risk discovery by having it shipped cross-country? Perhaps she believed in the old saying that you should keep your friends close and your enemies, even the dead ones, closer. We'll never know for sure, because that was one question she declined to answer before passing. Only the murder itself was too much for her to keep quiet about. That secret was simply too big to take to the grave.

PART

III

LAWN OF THE DEAD

Grave misunderstandings concerning
corpses that, though buried, refused
to rest in peace.

THE BACKYARD BONEYARD

Indianapolis-area residents Herb and Julie Baumeister seemed to live the American dream. They owned a successful business, had three kids, and resided in Fox Hollow Farms, a la-di-da development in one of the most gentrified sections of the city's northern suburbs. Their home was a sprawling, Tudor-style behemoth surrounded by acres of forest.

Everything looked perfect. And for Herb, it probably was. The business generated the cash he needed to live a secret double life. The family provided a perfect cover. And the woods on his property were an excellent spot to dump the bodies of his many, many victims.

Because Herb, we know now, had a hobby. To the outside world he was a mild-mannered businessman. Little did anyone realize—until it was too late—that he was also a serial killer.

Born in 1947, he led a life that, until the very end, seemed utterly

> Attention, serial killers: If you dump corpses on your own property, make sure you bury them deep.

innocuous. Even his face and physique were forgettable—medium build, medium height, not ugly, but not overly handsome. In other words, a police sketch artist's nightmare. He married his wife, Julie, in 1971, started a family, and opened two thriving thrift stores. They were so successful that they allowed the couple to purchase their Fox Hollow Farms home in 1991.

It was great for a growing brood, and great for other things as well. Every summer Herb packed his wife and kids off to an out-of-state lakeside condo while he stayed behind "to work." Apparently, from what police can surmise, he was mostly working the local gay bars. He would pick up young men, take them to his house, strangle them, then bury them in his yard—some no more than fifteen feet (4.5 m) from his back door. He became so careless that in 1994 his thirteen-year-old son actually stumbled across a human skull, along with some other bones, and reported it to his mother. In an almost unbelievable display of intestinal fortitude (and gullibility on the part of his wife), Herb fast-talked himself out of trouble by claiming the bones were pieces of an articulated skeleton that had belonged to his father, an anesthesiologist. He said he'd found it a while back while cleaning out the garage, and—as *anyone* would do if they chanced upon a human skeleton—had simply hauled it out and tossed it into the woods.

The fact that no one challenged this whopper was an incredible stroke of luck. But then Herb seemed to have a talent for explaining things away—and for simply being overlooked. For years, the Indianapolis Police Department had been aware of reports of missing gay men, but their investigations were cursory, to put it mildly. The cops, if they thought about it at all, figured the men had simply lit out on short notice for parts unknown. Certainly the words "serial killer" never came up. In the midnineties, an informant came forward to say that he'd visited the Hamilton County home of a man who first attempted to strangle him, then waxed poetic about the joy of erotic asphyxiation (strangling someone during sex to heighten the experience). But the big break was fumbled when the victim, to whom Baumeister gave a fake name, couldn't remember the location of the house.

But Herb's skill at going undetected would soon fail him. In the summer of 1995, the same man who made it out of the Baumeister house alive spotted his would-be killer at a gay bar and managed to get the license plate of his vehicle. It belonged to Herb, all right, but the police still didn't have a reason to arrest him—or to get a search warrant for his home, for that matter.

Not that there weren't other ways of getting what they wanted.

Initially, both Herb and Julie refused to talk to police or to allow them on their property. But Julie became distinctly more pliable once the beans were spilled about her supposedly devoted husband's nocturnal ramblings. And just as their marriage headed for the rocks, the Baumeisters' business tanked as well. With foreclosure on his

Police combed Herb Baumeister's property for months to piece together the serial killer's handiwork.

mortgage looming and a disgruntled wife who was no longer inclined to stonewall the cops, Herb knew it was only a matter of time before forensics experts got the run of the place and started digging up his yard work.

The dam finally broke in June 1996, when Julie split with Herb, sat down for a police interview, and agreed to allow a search of her home's grounds. Almost immediately the investigators found bones— bones on the ground, bones in shallow graves, bones in the woods far from the house, and bones almost at the family's doorstep. After weeks of going over the place with a fine-tooth comb, the cops found seven bodies, only four of which could be identified.

Of course, Herb could have named them all, had he cared to. Instead, as soon as he realized the jig was up, he skipped town and fled to Canada. There, he wrote a suicide note in which he blamed his troubles on his crumbling marriage and business reversals. He said nothing about his other activities. Then he drove to a park area and blew his brains out in his car.

But even though Herb was dead, his body count kept rising. He'd spent the early nineties turning the property around his home into a graveyard. But what had he done during the eighties, when he'd lived a more modest life that didn't include such wonderful serial killer conveniences as a big, secluded piece of property? Apparently he'd had to be more creative. In the years following Herb's demise, police pinned a further nine murders of Indianapolis-area homosexuals on him. The bodies of those victims, all of whom were killed during the pre–Fox Hollow Farm days, had been found in shallow streams across central Indiana and western Ohio. All had been strangled.

Apparently, according to associates, back in those days Herb took regular "business trips." It wasn't until years after the fact that people realized what his business really was.

CONCRETE EVIDENCE

Dean Faiello was a lot like his house. To a casual observer, his Greek revival mansion in Newark's elite Forest Hill section looked like a veritable shrine to financial success. And Faiello, a Madison, New Jersey, native who'd made a great deal of money in the beauty business, seemed like just the sort of person who would reside in such a place.

But appearances can be deceiving.

In some cases, murderously so.

As his neighbors and work associates knew, there was something not quite right about either Faiello or his domicile. The house, surrounded by a forbidding iron fence, was neglected and slowly falling into disrepair. Its owner was likewise falling to pieces. His carefully constructed facade of financial success was slipping, revealing a drug-addicted poser in deep trouble with the law. But no one knew just how much trouble he was in, save for him. Which was why, with foreclosure on his mansion looming, he'd decid-

When a fake MD committed a very real murder, he used a "home improvement" job to hide his not-so-handy work.

The garage of the Newark home where Dean Faiello
buried the corpse of his "patient."

ed in April 2003 to put the place on the market and get out of town.

Day in and day out, Faiello, assisted by his longtime lover, Greg Bach, and a neighbor named Mark Ritchie, spruced up the imposing structure to ready it for sale. Actually, the work involved a lot more than simple sprucing. The foundation had to be patched, and various other structural issues needed to be addressed. But Faiello, who had briefly worked in construction, seemed up to the task. He was particularly eager to fix the floor of the garage and asked Bach to pick up some extra bags of concrete at Home Depot for just that purpose. The task was so important that, on the night before the sale closed, Bach was surprised to find Faiello in the garage, working feverishly on the project.

His reaction to being seen was memorable, to say the least. According to media reports, the flabbergasted Bach said his lover shouted, "Get the hell out of here. Go do something else."

Not surprisingly, this overreaction at being caught in the middle of what looked like a routine concrete patch job left a big impression. Bach filed the encounter away in his memory bank. After the house

After fleeing to Costa Rica, Faiello was fetched back
to the United States to face murder charges.

closing, Faiello first left New York, then left the country in September.
The two men never saw each other again.

But though he couldn't have known it, picking up those bags of
cement made Bach an unwitting accomplice to murder. Or, perhaps
more accurately, to Faiello's attempt to cover up a killing. An attempt
that might have been successful had Bach not witnessed that late-night
concrete work—and had Faiello's reaction not been so overblown. The
encounter was still fresh in Bach's mind months later when police
came calling, asking about the disappearance of thirty-five-year-old
financial analyst Maria Cruz.

Cruz had been a classic immigrant success story, moving to the
United States from the Philippines, putting herself through Fordham
University's business school (where she graduated with honors), and
landing a posh job at Barclays Capital, where she pulled down around
$200,000 a year. She seemed to have everything going for her. That is,

right up until April 13, 2003, when she went to church, checked in at her office, and then, for all intents and purposes, vanished from the surface of the earth.

What wouldn't be known for months was that Cruz had an afternoon appointment to see Faiello about a condition she'd developed called black tongue—a painless, discolored growth that is sometimes caused by antibiotic use. Cruz, apparently, had employed Faiello to treat the problem—a fairly straightforward procedure for any doctor versed in the disorder.

And there was the rub. Faiello was neither versed in the disorder, nor a doctor.

Not that he informed Cruz of this, or any of his other "patients." For years the man had either told people, or allowed them to believe, that he was an MD. The charade began years earlier, when Faiello first moved to New York City. After trying his hand at construction, he became involved in the cosmetology industry, where he worked as a highly paid hair removal specialist. A veteran partier, he met Bach in 1998. The two started living together, primarily at Faiello's Newark mansion.

But the beauty biz magnate also had a substance abuse problem. In 1998, he was busted for using a stolen prescription pad to get drugs for himself. Even worse, Bach began to suspect that his lover was passing himself off as a doctor. He was actually performing procedures, such as laser tattoo removal, that in New York can only be undertaken by a physician. In October 2002, he was finally busted for practicing medicine without a license.

Faiello managed to get a light sentence by agreeing to rat out other quacks. But he couldn't break the habit himself. Even while he awaited sentencing, he started playing doctor again out of a friend's Manhattan apartment. It was during this time that, for some reason, he crossed paths with Maria Cruz. On the afternoon of April 13, 2003, the fumbling former hair removal specialist did something to try to fix her oral infection. Something that killed her.

After some six months of investigations, the New York police finally learned that Cruz had seen Faiello at least once a month since January

2003, and that she'd scheduled an appointment with him on the evening of her disappearance. Unfortunately, they couldn't find the "doctor" himself. So they settled for Bach.

Needless to say, his opinion of his former lover, who blew town owing him tens of thousands of dollars, had soured since Faiello's departure. Now he was confronted with evidence that the man he'd lived with for years might be a murderer. Stunned, he instantly recalled the strange business with the garage and the wet cement. Why, exactly, was it so important to fix that floor? A floor that hadn't seemed to need fixing?

Perhaps, it finally dawned on Bach, the home handyman had been hiding a problem rather than repairing one.

That was all the cops needed to hear. Using jackhammers, they ripped out the fake doctor's handiwork, exposing a large suitcase containing the decomposing corpse of Maria Cruz. Police surmise that she'd reacted adversely to a dose of lidocaine—mainly because that evening Faiello frantically called two real doctors, asking what to do in such a situation. Apparently he decided to do nothing, allowing his "patient" to expire. Then he stuffed her body in a suitcase, hauled it home, and got busy out in the garage.

Faiello, who in the meantime had fled to Costa Rica, was now a fugitive. After a prolonged extradition fight (financed, primarily, by the proceeds from the sale of his house), he was hauled back to New York to face second-degree murder charges. It seems that when it came to playing doctor or playing home handyman, he just couldn't do anything right.

GRAVEYARD SHIFT

Even the choicest real estate may contain unsavory secrets hidden just below the surface.

The Newport subdivision, located just outside of Houston, Texas, was supposed to be a homeowner's dream. Its upscale abodes were platted on scenic, unspoiled land on the edge of the city—close enough to make commuting a breeze, but far enough away to insulate it from the noise and grime of the urban core.

Newport's residents should have been on easy street. But there was just one problem. The land they built on may have been empty, but it was by no means unoccupied. And they would discover at great personal cost that the original inhabitants didn't take kindly to newcomers.

The horror began in the early 1980s, when the neighborhood's first families moved into their dream homes. Almost from the moment they arrived, Ben and Jean Williams sensed something was wrong. Their scratch-built house was perfect, and the landscaping beautiful. But for some reason the couple couldn't shake the feeling that they were being watched. Nor could they escape a miasma of melancholy and menace that seemed to hang over them. And there were other, more practical, problems as well. The toilets flushed on their own, the lights flickered on and off for no good reason, the garage door rose and fell unbidden, and far too many poisonous snakes seemed to find their way into their yard.

Soon their neighbors reported similarly odd problems—and similar feelings of unease. There was something about the landscape that didn't seem right. A tree in the Williamses' backyard was covered with strange markings, and the property was dotted with unusual, rectangular sinkholes that seemed to form a pattern. But the Newport families didn't truly comprehend the horror of their situation until 1983, when Sam and Judith Haney started excavating their backyard to install a pool. Almost immediately, their contractor uncovered a pair of old, rotted coffins containing the bodies of a man and a woman.

This was only a foretaste of the unsettling revelations to come. After a great deal of sleuthing, the distraught Newport families came into contact with Jasper Norton, an elderly black man formerly employed as a grave digger. He said he knew the neighborhood well, because it was built on top of a cemetery called Black Hope. As many as sixty people, many of them former slaves, were interred right under the Williamses' and the Haneys' feet. Norton identified the bodies in the Haneys' backyard as those of Betty and Charlie Thomas, former slaves who died in the 1930s.

The Haneys were, naturally, horrified, but out of respect for the dead made the extraordinary decision to rebury the Thomases in their back-yard. But apparently, the damage had already been done. Right after the relocation and reburial, the Haney house was made almost unlivable by marauding ghosts. Disembodied voices and footsteps echoed through the halls. An unplugged clock in the bedroom started to glow eerily and shoot sparks. On one particularly memorable evening, Judith heard the ground-level sliding glass door open and close. Figuring it was her husband returning from work, she padded downstairs to find no one home.

The next morning she couldn't locate a pair of red shoes. She finally found them outdoors—sitting neatly on top of Betty Thomas's grave.

Similar encounters were reportedly happening up and down Newport's formerly bucolic streets. Not surprisingly, the neighborhood began to empty as terrified homeowners decided to cut and run rather than face the ever-more-disturbing, ever-more-dangerous manifestations taking place all around them. But the Haneys stayed, as did their across-the-street neighbors, the Williams family. They would pay a terrible price for their stubbornness.

At the Williamses' home, the problems had progressed far beyond such annoyances as flushing toilets and flickering lights. The couple's granddaughter, Carli, had become physically ill. And rectangular, grave-shaped sinkholes opened up in their lawn. The couple would fill them in with fresh dirt, only to have them reappear in the same spots days later. Indoors, disembodied footsteps rang through the rooms. And one night Ben reportedly came home to find a strange apparition hovering over his sleeping wife.

The Haneys were likewise at the end of their rope. Plagued, like the Williams family, by inexplicable health problems, they filed a lawsuit against the neighborhood's developer for not disclosing what would have been, to any sane person, a deal-breaking problem. The couple was awarded a settlement by a jury, but the judge reversed the decision. Defeated, the Haneys declared bankruptcy and simply walked away from their home.

They weren't the first Newport residents to do so, and they wouldn't be the last.

The Williams family still clung to their property, and it was they who would pay the highest price for their stubbornness. The couple, who had also contemplated legal action against the developer, was desperate to find evidence to support them. They thought they found it when a longtime resident of the area told them that the strange scratches on an old oak tree in their backyard—a downward-pointing arrow with two slash marks beneath it—marked the spot where two sisters were buried.

And so Jean, in an effort to establish once and for all that her house was built over a cemetery, started digging at one of the sinkholes near the tree. Soon she became so exhausted by the effort that her thirty-year-old daughter, Tina, took over. But after perhaps half an hour of exertion, Tina collapsed from a massive heart attack. She died two days later.

That was enough for the distraught Williams family. They, too, abandoned the cursed neighborhood and moved far away, to Montana. By all reports, they now live a blessedly ghost-free existence. As for the neighborhood itself, the current residents say they haven't had any problems. Perhaps, after indirectly causing one untimely death, the spirits finally decided that enough was enough.

FROZEN ASSET

The residents of Nederland, Colorado, are living proof of the old adage "When life hands you lemons, make lemonade." Only in this case, life handed them not tart citrus fruit, but the frozen corpse of an elderly Norwegian gentleman. From this grisly discovery the locals created a publicity bonanza that's put this town just outside of Denver on the map—at least for one weekend each winter, when it hosts a macabre but memorable little soiree called Frozen Dead Guy Days.

A dead Norwegian man becomes a small town's most lively civic booster.

It all began on a decidedly less festive note, back in Norway on November 6, 1989. That's when lifelong resident Bredo Morstoel died quietly in his sleep at the age of eighty-eight. But instead of laying the body to rest, his grandson, Trygve Bauge (who had lived in Boulder, Colorado, since 1980), decided to have him preserved with an eye toward reviving him at some point in the future. So the corpse was packed in dry ice and shipped to a company in Oakland, California, where poor Morstoel was placed in a steel coffin and immersed in bitterly cold liquid nitrogen for nearly four years. Then, in 1993, he was moved from Oakland to Nederland.

Bauge, who was interested in the field of cryonics (freezing dead people in hopes of someday resurrecting them), wanted to open his own facility there and had purchased some land for the purpose. Grandpa was to be the first client. But shortly after the corpse was moved to a metal shed on the property, Bauge, who was in the United States on an expired visa, was deported back to Norway. Not long afterward, his mother, Aud, was evicted from the Nederland property and, because she also carried an expired visa, sent home. But before departing, she told a local reporter about the dead body and her fears that in her absence it would be allowed to thaw.

When local authorities visited the site, they found not one but two corpses, the other being that of an individual identified only as "Al," who was apparently the second client of Bauge's budding cryonics company. When Al's family members were informed, the body was shipped out and buried.

Which left only Grandpa. According to the local paper, the *Daily Camera*, when Nederland mayor Bryan Brown learned of the discovery, he said, "I feel like I'm in a David Lynch movie."

Plenty of news organizations agreed. The situation ignited a blaze of

The temporary resting place of "Grandpa" Bredo Morstoel.

publicity back in 1994, when media from around the world descended on the tiny town. The horrified residents quickly passed an ordinance making it illegal to keep dead humans or parts of dead humans on one's property. However, because Morstoel was already there, he was granted a grandfather clause that allowed him to stay. Indeed, he became an unofficial mascot of sorts. The rickety shed he was kept in was replaced with a sturdier structure. Every four or five weeks, a technician replenishes the dry ice that keeps the steel coffin chilled. The roughly $700-a-month price tag is covered by the ever-faithful Trygve and Aud.

It wasn't until eight years after the original discovery, however, that the Nederland Area Chamber of Commerce decided they could turn the frozen corpse in their midst into a public relations gold mine. Deciding it was time to reanimate the story of Grandpa, they inaugurated Frozen Dead Guy Days in 2002, a late-winter festival in March that draws around eight thousand people. "Festivities" include coffin races, an excruciatingly painful-sounding variant of the wet T-shirt contest called the frozen T-shirt contest, a Grandpa look-alike pageant (presumably premortem), a champagne tour of the shed housing the postanimate (if you're a pessimist) or preanimate (if you're an optimist) remains of Bredo Morstoel, and a not-the-least-bit-disrespectful-sounding dance called Grandpa's Blue Ball. "It's like one of those things that never goes away, like a mole," local resident Teresa Warren told the *Daily Camera*. "People now associated Nederland with a frozen dead guy, and we can't make it disappear, so why not create an economic opportunity for our town?"

Why not, indeed. If you think about it, perhaps not too deeply, is it any stranger than the festival in nearby Fruita, Colorado, honoring Mike the Headless Chicken, an unfortunate rooster who survived for years after having his head chopped off? Well, perhaps it's just a *shade* stranger, when you throw in the fact that the town installed viewing stands around the shed so folks could get a better look at Grandpa. Or that the chamber of commerce Web site offers a full line of Frozen Dead Guy souvenirs, from hats to posters to T-shirts.

But that's okay. Capitalism is capitalism, and you've got to do whatever it takes to grease the wheels of commerce. The town of Nederland may be hopping during Frozen Dead Guy Days, but the rest of the year it's pretty much dead—just like its most famous resident.

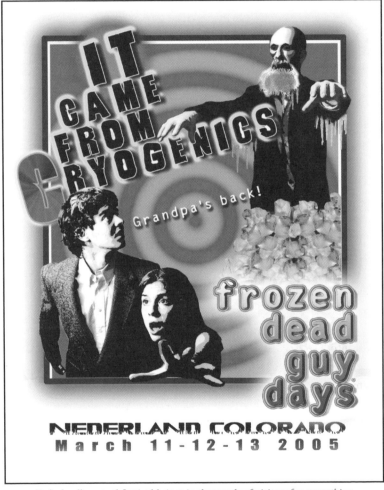

Nederland's annual festival brings in thousands of visitors for everything from coffin races to a dance. Yes, there are souvenir T-shirts.

ARMY OF DARKNESS

It's hard to imagine a town less inclined to evil than Wausau, Wisconsin. Here the locals keep their lawns neat and their homes immaculate, and a wild night out usually entails either bratwursts on the grill or a road trip to nearby Green Bay for a Packers game. This just isn't the sort of place where one expects an assault from the undead.

Nothing can kill a home's resale potential like an Indian burial ground full of angry spirits.

And yet, if reports can be believed, that's just what happened in Wausau.

It all began in 1972, when Harry and Jackie Fischer purchased a split-level home in a sedate, perfectly innocuous subdivision. Then they settled in for what they figured would be a sedate, perfectly innocuous existence. Except that, for some reason, cookware stored in the kitchen cabinets inexplicably rattled and shook, and a mysterious ringing noise, as if from a tiny bell, seemed to waft through various rooms at odd times.

At first the couple gave these oddball occurrences little thought. But then whatever was vexing them suddenly decided to up the ante. Jackie's father came to visit, and one evening as he listened to the radio, the unit suddenly drifted off station and emitted a loud, high-pitched whine. That was disturbing. But not nearly as disturbing as what happened next. A lit candle on a nearby table slowly levitated, dipped over until it pointed at Jackie's father, then righted itself and settled back onto the table.

The couple could only roll their eyes when Jackie's father reported what happened. But soon, in true poltergeist fashion, household objects regularly started flying through the air. Plus, the family stereo continued to misbehave, changing stations and emitting the same high-pitched whine Jackie's father complained of. Repairmen checked the unit from top to bottom but couldn't find anything wrong.

The family's cocker spaniel also got in on the act. The house featured a narrow staircase just inside the front door that led up to the second floor and down to the cellar. The cocker, with unnerving regularity, would sit at the top of the cellar steps, stare down into the darkness, and growl at something that, apparently, only it could see. What it was, no one could say. But judging from the way the animal's hair stood on end, it clearly wasn't the tooth fairy.

All this was only a prelude to the main event. After about a year of weird but not necessarily sinister incidents, the couple had acclimated themselves to having an occasional coffee table knickknack tossed at them, and to their dog's obsession with the basement. But in 1973 the footsteps began. Late at night the couple would hear soft padding in the basement. Then the steps would creak up the stairs to the landing and onto the first floor before petering out. Night after night the same thing happened.

And night after night, the ghost that lived with them seemed to become more powerful, more assertive, and more aggressive. As with any "typical" haunting, doors opened and shut on their own and lights switched on and off. But one night as Jackie was preparing to shave her legs, her razor suddenly leaped into the air and shot past her head, missing her by inches. Clearly whatever they were dealing with could be dangerous.

During this time, the footsteps got so loud and so numerous that on some nights it sounded as if an army were marching through their house. Harry grew so agitated and sleep deprived that one evening he crept out of the master bedroom and flipped on the lights to catch the unseen entities in the act. But the joke was on him: The lights refused to work. The next morning, however, they functioned just fine.

Not long afterward, the fire department was summoned to quell a small blaze in the basement. After some head-scratching, they finally laid the blame on a battery charger—even though the Fischers swore up and down that it wasn't plugged in at the time. Later, while Jackie was washing clothes in the basement, she heard a thumping sound in the nearby storage room. But when she tried to open the door, something very large and very solid refused to allow her entry. She dashed up the stairs in terror, but when she returned with reinforcements later, the door opened without difficulty.

That was enough for the Fischers, who immediately put the house up for sale. Incredibly they were able to find another couple interested in buying the place—Jim and Mary Strasser. Even though they'd been told in blood-curdling detail about what had transpired in their soon-to-be home, they felt there must be a reasonable explanation and weren't afraid.

Unfortunately, their faith in reason was misplaced. As had happened with the Fischers, the ghostly manifestations they endured started out small, then got bigger and bigger. First there was a loud, persistent, almost human-sounding humming. A humming that vaguely resembled some sort of tribal rhythm. Then the usual tossing of objects and the relentless after-hours marching. Then, in a new and terrifying twist, the couple's young daughter reported that something squeezed her toes whenever she got into bed. And Jim Strasser reported a vivid nightmare in which he was an old Native American wrapped in a blanket who was slowly choking to death.

Perhaps the deus ex machina of hundreds of horror novels and films, an Indian burial ground, was at fault. Local historians have said that the subdivision where the Fischer/Strasser residence stands might formerly have been just such a place. If so, then the people who think they own that piece of property have no doubt angered the (long-deceased) people who really do.

ON DANGEROUS GROUND

How do you know if your neighbor is a serial killer? Examine his lawn.

One of the twentieth century's most vile serial murderers was the infamous Killer Clown, John Wayne Gacy. It's hard to imagine a more grotesque caricature of a human being. To his neighbors in the suburban town of Des Plaines, Illinois, he was a small-time contractor who could be quite likable when it suited him. He was active in the Jaycees, worked for the local Democratic Party machine, and even dressed up as a clown and performed at area children's parties.

But Gacy also enjoyed darker pursuits. From 1972 until he was finally cornered by police and confessed in 1978, he killed thirty-three young men, dumping five in the Des Plaines River and burying the other twenty-eight under his house and garage. Digging them up was a logistical nightmare for local officials, and it was an indescribable horror show for his neighbors. In the course of their weeks-long excavation, the cops leveled the Gacy home and garage and even jackhammered his patio, from which they extracted the well-preserved corpse of yet

Police and forensics experts cleaning up the mess at
John Wayne Gacy's charnel house.

another victim. Based in part on this bounty of evidence, Gacy was
tried and sentenced to death in 1980. That judgment was carried out
on May 9, 1994.

By the time of Gacy's sentencing, his charnel house had been annihilated. All that remained was a barren patch of dirt planted right in the
heart of a bustling middle-class neighborhood. But although almost
every bit of the old residence had been pulverized or carted away—
including the barbecue pit and driveway—the area still drew carloads
of sightseers, who cruised by at all hours.

Neighbors hoped that when the spring of 1980 arrived, the muddy
mess at what had once been 8213 West Summerdale would disappear
under the cover of rejuvenating greenery. But it didn't happen. The
warm weather came, but the grass didn't. For eighteen months after
the house was leveled, the spot where it and the garage stood reportedly remained bereft of vegetation. Police theorized that perhaps the

lime Gacy sprinkled on some of his victims had poisoned the soil. The problem was, he hadn't used all that much, and what he had used had been dispersed and diluted by backhoes that churned the ground to a depth of eight feet (2.4 m).

One is reminded of old European beliefs that grass will refuse to grow on the grave of a murdered person, as if nature itself is appalled by the crime. The macabre scene was finally erased several years later, when an intrepid soul purchased the parcel and built a new house on it. Though setting up one's domicile on the burial ground of a serial killer sounds about as promising as erecting a shopping mall

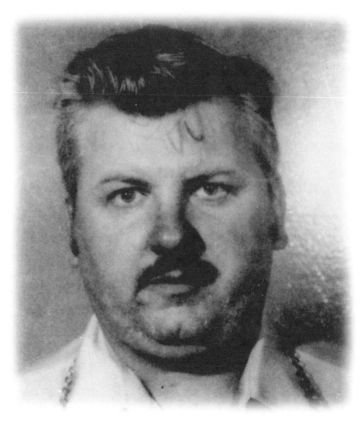

John Wayne Gacy

at a nuclear test site, things seem to have worked out. Once the new residence was built, its lawn sprouted grass again. The house at 8213 West Summerdale was "normal" once more. Except for the fact that there was no more 8213 West Summerdale. The new owners were so bent on exorcising past demons—and ending the gawking problem— that they had the address number changed.

HOME IMPROVEMENTS FROM HELL

Renovating a house can be a hassle under the best of circumstances. For Jefferson, Wisconsin, resident Helen Weisensel, it turned into a nightmare. The problem wasn't with faulty workmanship or zoning permits or tardy contractors. It was the corpses. All the darn corpses.

New homeowners could be sitting on an equity gold mine—unless they're sitting on a graveyard.

Weisensel owned her property for twenty years before she became aware that she had a zoning problem—namely, that her house sat in a legal and metaphysical twilight zone. The trouble began in 2003, when she embarked on an extensive remodeling scheme, including work on the foundation. She hired a man with a backhoe to move some earth, but only a few seconds after he broke ground, things got very, very complicated. "He only got a scoop and a half of dirt out, and when he dumped the second scoop, a human skull actually rolled out of the dirt," Weisensel told a local news outlet.

It turns out her house had been built on one of the town's old cemeteries. The graveyard had been moved years earlier, but as the evidence showed, not everybody got the memo. Bones of an adult and a child have been found, and there's no telling what else lurks under the sod.

Needless to say, the discovery threw a wrench into Weisensel's renovation scheme. She can't resume her work until the State Historical Society, which has been charged with protecting the integrity of a burial ground that no one knew was a burial ground, figures out how to proceed. Perhaps Weisensel can take some small comfort from the fact that the phenomenon of old cemeteries under new housing developments (the plot of the 1982 thriller *Poltergeist*) isn't an isolated problem. In 2004, Prescott, Arizona, resident Marylyn Lundgren unearthed a human skull while gardening in her backyard; and in the Wisconsin town of Orfordville, plans for a new office park ran afoul of a very old cemetery.

At least, unlike in *Poltergeist*, Weisensel hasn't faced any visitations from irritated spirits—like, say, from the guy who had his skull lopped off by the backhoe. "Everybody asks me that, you know, 'Did you have weird things happen in your home?'" she said. "I said, 'No, my house is just fine.'"

THE VANISHING PATTERSONS

A Texas couple who disappeared under peculiar circumstances may have been spies or UFO abductees. Or they may just be buried out in their yard somewhere.

El Paso residents William and Margaret Patterson were quiet, unassuming people. Certainly not the sort you'd expect to be Russian spies. Or UFO abductees. Or ghosts. But they've been accused, at various times and by various people, of being all three. Unfortunately, they can't set the record straight themselves. That's because one day the couple stepped out of their front door and, for all intents and purposes, fell right off the surface of the earth. "It's like they went out for a walk and never came back," El Paso County sheriff Leo Samaniego told the *El Paso Times*.

He's the most recent in a long string of lawmen who've spent many a fruitless hour trying to track the couple down. It all started—or, from the Pattersons' perspective, ended—on March 5 or 6, 1957. That was the last time anyone recalls seeing them either at their home in the 3000 block of Piedmont or at their downtown business, Patterson Photo Supply. There wasn't much concern at first, because they'd mentioned going to Florida. But weeks went by without a word from them. Finally, in August of that year, a family friend, Cecil Ward, filed a report with the sheriff's department about the disappearance. A search of the couple's house found nothing missing or out of place. Even their cat was still hanging around the property. Stymied by a lack of evidence, the cops at the time decided the duo had simply lit out for parts unknown.

But which parts? Almost any theory seemed plausible. Some thought they were snatched by kidnappers or abducted by a UFO. Others said they headed for Mexico. Or that they were Russian agents who'd been suddenly called home. Ironically, that theory still enjoys fairly wide acceptance in certain circles. "I think they were spies," asserted Samaniego in the *Times.* "The way they got up and just walked away and left everything behind. The Russians, or whoever sent them, probably told them to drop everything and go back. Some people said they had seen Patterson taking photographs of Fort Bliss and of military shipments on the trains that came here."

Well . . . okay. Perhaps they were enemy agents. Or perhaps, as others assert, they simply went someplace to start new lives. Back in the fifties, the same people who said the Pattersons went to Florida also claimed that they later sent word that they weren't coming back. Over the decades they were also supposedly sighted in Mexico. Early on, even William Patterson's father seemed to think that the couple had simply relocated without bothering to tell anyone. "I always knew Pat and Margaret would take off like this some day, but I figured it to be four or five years away," he told an El Paso court of inquiry. "They're not dead. . . . My boy has done things like this before. . . . He made his living doing sleight-of-hand tricks."

There was just one problem. Patterson's father never got so much as a birthday card from them. The silence was so profound that as the years passed he began to suspect that they were dead, not just gone.

Not surprisingly, their former abode quickly acquired a reputation for being haunted, a reputation it still enjoys today. The residents who set up housekeeping in the years after the disappearance were constantly calling the police to report disturbances. Not ghostly disturbances, but problems caused by teenagers sneaking around, looking for spirits.

Actually, those kids might have had a point. A certain segment of the locals have always believed the Pattersons never went anywhere, and that they can still be found on—or rather, beneath—the grounds of their property. Former El Paso County Sheriff R. L. "Bob" Bailey told the *El Paso Herald-Post* that "at one time Frank [Morning, the chief sheriff's deputy in charge of the 1950s investigation] thought maybe the bodies were buried right there in or under the house, but he could never find any evidence of it."

That is, until 1984. That year the police heard from a man named Reynaldo Nangaray, who had been hired to look after the Patterson place shortly after their disappearance. In his official statement, Nangaray said he'd found blood in the garage and a piece of human scalp on the propeller of the couple's boat, which was stored on the premises. Even more telling, he said he witnessed one of the Pattersons' friends removing bloody sheets from the house and stashing them in the trunk of a car. "He did not come forward to talk to the police sooner because he was an illegal immigrant at the time, but when he came to see us, he was a U.S. citizen," reports former El Paso Police Department homicide detective (and now private investigator) Freddie Bonilla.

Unfortunately, Mr. Nangaray won't be shedding any further light on the matter. He died in a car accident two years after telling his curious tale to police.

Which leaves investigators exactly where they were in 1957—without a clue. Every few years, the El Paso police haul out the dusty files and take another swing at the case. But as the decades pass, the trail gets colder and colder, even as the Legend of the Vanishing Pattersons looms larger and larger.

Where did the couple go? Maybe they're in Mexico or Russia or in the belly of a UFO. Or maybe they didn't go anywhere. Maybe they're still at their house, waiting to be found. Only one thing is certain. Until they're found, their case will continue to haunt the city of El Paso.

GROUND-BREAKING DISCOVERY

As anyone who reads cheesy horror novels or watches a lot of old *X-Files* reruns already knows, an Indian burial ground is the worst place in the world to build a home, with the possible exception of a Superfund site or a decommissioned minefield. Unfortunately, clueless homeowners rarely realize what they've done until after the papers are signed and the down

Often homeowners don't find out they're sitting on haunted territory until it's too late. But not always.

payment changes hands. Then, when the walls start dripping blood and creepy, disembodied voices waft up from the basement, it's too late to do anything but dodge the flying crockery and watch their resale value plummet.

And, perhaps, to pack a couple of suitcases for that inevitable moment when the whole family flees, screaming, in the middle of the night.

Thankfully, this won't be the case for those intrepid few who choose to build their dream houses in an upscale San Francisco–area development called Hidden Oaks. Anyone who purchases space in this thirteen-and-a-half-acre (5.5 hectare) parcel will never have to suffer a moment's uncertainty as to whether or not their home rests atop an Indian burial ground.

Mainly because an entire squad of archaeologists has already proven that it absolutely, positively does.

And a big one at that. Apparently the area now called Hidden Oaks has always been a choice slice of real estate. The land sits where two creeks converge—a very auspicious sign that made it perfect for living and, of course, burying. All of this happened roughly a millennium ago, before anyone could conceive of a Bay Area real estate bubble so vast that it would send speculators scrambling to plant McMansions on every bit of land they could lay hands on.

Which brings us back to Hidden Oaks.

Unfortunately for its developers, the discovery of human remains constitutes just one more problem in a long list of difficulties. The plan to shoehorn yet another batch of houses into the area was fought by the current inhabitants. Plus, the company doing the job, Smith Quality Homes, had to pony up just shy of $1 million to study the archaeological impact of all its digging and paving. And now, of course, many of the firm's hard hats are simply standing around, waiting for a team of archaeologists to make sense of what they've stumbled across.

Not that they shouldn't have expected something like this. The land has been considered an archaeological site for more than one hundred years. Indeed, homeowners in surrounding areas have routinely turned up bones and other artifacts while installing tennis courts and swimming pools.

But what the bulldozers uncovered in Hidden Oaks in June 2004 was different. Mostly because there was so much more. "I would not be surprised if in the inner Bay Area . . . I never saw another one of this caliber for the rest of my career," Allen Pastron, an urban archaeologist for the city of Oakland who is leading the dig, told the *San Francisco Chronicle*.

The find, which stopped work on roughly two acres (.8 hectares) of the property, included about fifty sets of human remains, all laid out reverently by an aboriginal people who, no doubt, would be very surprised and upset if they knew what had happened to their ancestors' supposedly eternal resting place. The stunningly complete site is also loaded with cultural artifacts, including everything from tools to beads to foodstuffs. Most of these have been trucked off to a secret location for more study. Not surprisingly, the archaeologists are keeping the details close to their vests for fear that looters might try to steal whatever they leave behind.

At some point, the remains will probably, under the guidance of a member of California's Native American Heritage Commission, be studied and then reinterred somewhere nearby. "In a perfect world what they should do is redesign the project," Native American Heritage Commission executive secretary Larry Myers told the *Chronicle*. "Can't we honor the burials that are here by putting them in a park or something?"

Not in today's tight real estate market. Smith Quality Homes is eager to continue, and potential buyers are still lining up, in spite of the macabre discoveries. Apparently they're not bothered (yet) by the fact that when they back their SUVs into their new garages and barbecue on their just-poured patios, they'll do so under the eyes of literally dozens of deceased—and recently displaced—Native Americans.

As anyone who's watched a horror movie (or has read the stories beginning on pages 187 and 195 in this book) already understands, this is what's known in paranormal circles as "asking for it." But at least, if the walls do start bleeding, they can't say they weren't warned.

PART
III

SUNDRY CUL-DE-SACRILEGES

Suburban horrors so bizarre they defy not
only explanation, but categorization

GHOSTS "R" US

Pity the morning crew at the Sunnyvale, California, Toys "R" Us. Often the folks who unlock the sprawling superstore at the crack of dawn find the previous evening's tidying and restocking undone by an unknown entity. Balls, games, and action figures, tucked away neatly only hours before, lie scattered in the aisles. And that's

At one California toy store, a ghostly staff member never punches out.

not all. This scourge of the stock workers is also active during business hours. Employees report hearing voices when no one's around and having their hair stroked by invisible fingers. The water faucets in the women's bathroom turn on and off by themselves. And aisle 15C sometimes smells like fresh flowers.

But why would a ghost bother haunting a place like Sunnyvale, an idyllic-looking community thirty miles south of San Francisco? And why would it make its presence felt in a toy store, of all places?

The most popular theory was put forward years ago by private psychic counselor Sylvia Brown. These days she's a fixture on Montel Williams's talk show, but back in the late seventies, she agreed to conduct an after-hours séance to try to get to the bottom of the terror at the toy store. According to Brown, the ghost is one John Johnson, a circuit preacher who worked in the Sunnyvale area back in the late 1800s, when the land on which the store stands was an apple orchard. He fell in love with the daughter of a local rancher, but his love wasn't returned. Johnson (nicknamed "Yonny" by store employees) met his end when he fatally injured himself with an ax while chopping wood.

The séance that divined all this information also produced another, more tangible artifact. Someone snapped a photo of the proceedings— a fuzzy black-and-white image that shows the participants sitting in a circle on the floor while a tall, shadowy figure stands leaning against the shelving behind them, observing. That figure, they figured, was Johnson himself, because apparently no one in their group stood there when the shot was taken.

Now, allegedly, poor Yonny walks the aisles of the Sunnyvale Toys "R" Us, bemoaning his lost love, slapping around Strawberry Shortcake dolls, fiddling with the plumbing fixtures, and touching staffers inappropriately. Although life (and the afterlife) seems to have dealt Mr. Johnson a bad hand, he hasn't taken it out on the living by doing anything truly violent or scary. As a matter of fact, the management might give him Employee of the Month honors if they could figure out a way to hand him the certificate. Having a member of the undead wandering the retail establishment has been very good for business. "Sales go up after reports of the ghost," assistant store director Jeff Linden told *Adweek's Marketing Week*. "A lot of people think this is a great thing."

NOISE POLLUTION

The town of Kokomo, Indiana, ought to be a fairly quiet place. Located about an hour down the road from the state capital of Indianapolis, it was formerly a bustling center for the automotive industry. Not long ago, the entire town rumbled with the sound of factories. This is the spot where everything from the pneumatic tire to stainless steel was invented.

But that was a long time ago. Many of the auto plants have been idled. These days the small city of forty-six thousand people is much quieter.

Or at least it ought to be.

The residents of a formerly quiet community must contend with a strange humming sound that plagues them day and night.

Even though Kokomo has never been more placid, it's never had more complaints about noise. Or, more specifically, about a peculiar hum. For almost a decade, a portion of the local population has complained about hearing a low, almost subsonic rumbling. It plagues them day and night, they say, and it's so relentless that it's caused everything from emotional trauma to physical ailments such as acute nausea and joint pain.

But the really weird part is that, while the roughly one hundred or so citizens who claim to hear the hum are driven absolutely batty by it, most of the Kokomo citizenry senses nothing at all. The problem surfaced in 1999, when a select group of locals reported noticing a low-pitched rumbling sound that some compared to an idling diesel engine and others to the incessant warble of a fluorescent bulb. But while descriptions of the sound differed, all who heard it agreed on one thing: It was making them physically ill or, at the very least, depriving them of sleep and slowly driving them to distraction.

But what really aggravated the hum's victims was the fact that almost no one took them seriously. The majority of Kokomo's residents, who remained blessedly unperturbed, often greeted complaints about strange sounds with, at best, bemused smiles. And state authorities, when contacted, could be even less helpful. The *Indianapolis Star* stated that when Maureen Christie tried to report hearing a loud, booming sound to the Indiana State Board of Health, she was told to go out in her yard and check for meteorites.

At least the local newshounds aren't laughing. The *Kokomo Tribune* published an extensive report on the subject, interviewing dozens of hum sufferers in the process. Many had seen doctors about their problems, but the physicians attributed their difficulties to everything from simple stress to the aging process. In the end, the *Tribune* called for an investigation into the matter. Gael Deppert, an Indianapolis attorney advising the victims, said pretty much the same thing. "We need to bring in scientists knowledgeable in various fields to try to grapple with this situation," she told the *Star*. "We're asking the state to come in with an open mind."

So far the state hasn't come in at all, open-minded or not. In part because there's no money for such a thing, but also because it's unclear just what sort of expert or experts possess skills germane to the topic. Kokomo itself recently funded a small study that found that low-frequency sounds emanated from two local factories. The scientists responsible for the work also theorized that, perhaps, cell phone towers might contribute in some way to the problem. Though of course nothing is certain.

At least Kokomo's hum-afflicted residents can take comfort in the fact that they aren't alone. Far from it. Communities afflicted with bizarre, droning sounds dot the globe, from Scotland to Japan to Scandinavia to Vancouver, British Columbia. But the most famous case by far is the Taos Hum, which afflicts people in northern New Mexico, but primarily the picturesque arts community of Taos. Just as in Kokomo, a small subset of the locals complained of hearing an omnipresent noise that robbed them of both their health and their peace of mind. But after years of worldwide publicity and a number of studies, the city understands exactly as much about the roots of the problem as they did a decade ago: nothing.

And perhaps most disheartening of all, the folks who heard the insidious noise back then are still hearing it now. Just like the long-suffering victims of the Kokomo Hum.

YOU WANT FRIGHTS WITH THAT?

A haunted McDonald's served its patrons a biggie-sized dose of terror from the deep-fryer of doom.

The typical McDonald's, like so many other fast-food joints, is housed in a mostly prefabricated building designed to be tossed up on a street corner in no time flat. That not-so-proud architectural tradition was broken when the chain located an eatery in the upstate New York resort town of Lewiston. Instead of parking yet another interchangeable French fry factory on a vacant lot with good traffic flow, the company set up shop inside a centuries-old building that formerly housed an inn and restaurant known as the Frontier House.

It was a bold, visionary move. And it's one that more than a few employees lived to regret.

Apparently the chain's new location came with more than just built-in atmosphere. It was also haunted. Really, really haunted. It seems that the old Frontier House is filled with ectoplasmic residue left over from the part it played in one of the nineteenth century's most famous disappearances.

It happened in 1826, when a low-level Freemason named William Morgan decided to write a book exposing the secret social club. Back in the 1820s, this was a big deal. Freemasonry was a closed society filled with arcane rites performed behind locked doors. In many communities, almost every person of note was a member—including George Washington, Thomas Jefferson, and Benjamin Franklin. Of course, now we know that all these men did was hang around in dusty meeting halls, make up secret handshakes, and entertain each other with silly rituals. But at the time, there was a growing suspicion in America that the Freemasons were up to something.

This made Morgan's book a potential bombshell—and a thorn in the side of the Freemasons. In September 1826, while he was still working on the manuscript, he was arrested twice—first for petty theft, then for failure to pay a small debt. While he languished in a jail cell, a group of men showed up, paid his fine, and hustled Morgan onto a coach bound for Fort Niagara. Reportedly, the party stayed overnight at the Frontier House en route. What happened after that is anybody's guess, because Morgan was never seen again. Enemies of Freemasonry figured he'd been taken away and disposed of. No one ever knew for sure, because his body was never discovered and the people who rode on the coach with Morgan took the secret to their graves.

Not surprisingly, locals figured it was Morgan the Mason who enlivened things at the Lewiston McDonald's. In the 1970s, the restaurant's manager complained of hearing strange, disembodied voices and seeing floating apparitions. A maintenance man quit after sighting a ghost, and a female custodian claimed that a milky-white old man regularly materialized in the pantry.

Perhaps Morgan enjoyed his stay at the Frontier House so much that, once he was relieved of his mortal form, he decided to come back and settle down. His presence was so widely accepted that the

McDonald's served as a centerpiece for a walking tour of Lewiston's haunted places.

Maybe his ghostly aura also helped speed the demise of the eatery, which recently closed its doors. It's quite an unexpected development, given that running a McDonald's out of business is usually harder than killing a cockroach. One wonders if the building's bad mojo was too much even for the all-conquering Golden Arches. The hoary structure remains and is being converted into an inn—something that will perhaps be more to the liking of the restless spirits that hold the place in thrall.

But even though the restaurant is gone, local legend holds that you can still have a spirit encounter just by hanging around the general area. Nearby Ridge Road, which Morgan's abductors traveled to get to the Frontier House, is said to be haunted by the sound of invisible, galloping horses hauling an unseen coach. No word on if they ever tried the McDonald's drive-through.

WATER, WATER EVERYWHERE

The trials of one Ohio family give new meaning to the phrase "water torture."

Even after more than thirty years, no one's come up with a solid explanation for what happened in the home of Clyde and Ann Frederick of Ayersville, Ohio, during one very eventful, very soggy July week in 1975. For six days and five nights, they were vexed by a strange phenomenon never seen before or since. To this day, no expert on the planet can say if the unfortunate family was persecuted by some ghostly entity with a bizarre sense of humor or simply beset by bad plumbing.

The saga began on a muggy Saturday, when the Fredericks and their kids, Julie and Danny, made an all-day visit to a friend's house. When they returned home that night, they found their kitchen floor inexplicably covered with several inches of water. They cleaned it up, but new puddles soon formed elsewhere. And not just on floors. Moisture accumulated on top of the TV, on shelves, even in drawers.

New patches of wetness appeared as soon as the frazzled family mopped up the old ones. Not surprisingly, the Fredericks were more than a little creeped out. Especially since the water always seemed to gather when they weren't looking. "It's hard to catch it forming, which only makes it more mysterious," Ann told the Defiance, Ohio, *Crescent-News*. "We only saw it form once—we could see the carpet get wet in a ring. It makes you nervous. It's worse because no one can tell us what's causing it."

Not that people didn't try. Plumbers said it wasn't any sort of leak. And since the ceiling, walls, and attic remained bone-dry, it wasn't coming in through the roof. Meteorologists and a city water official allowed that it might be caused by condensation, though they were at a loss to explain how the problem could be so severe, and why it would manifest itself in such odd places.

The Frederick family doggedly battled the rising tide, covering their possessions with plastic sheets, enlisting neighbors and relatives to help with mopping, and removing kitchen and bedroom drawers after they filled repeatedly with water. Not surprisingly, people started to wonder if supernatural rather than natural causes were to blame. The talk got stronger as the days passed and the waterlogged goings-on showed no signs of stopping. Robert Easley, a resident of the nearby town of Defiance and editor of *Flying Saucer Digest*, proposed that the trouble might be caused by a water poltergeist. He then offered a seventeenth-century exorcism rite and the recipe for a magic potion involving John the Conqueror root and sycamore chips.

At that point, the Fredericks were too tired and stressed to care if their trouble was meteorological or metaphysical. Their garage was unaffected, so many of their most vulnerable possessions were piled there. At night they got up every hour on the hour to look for fresh pools. But finally, at 3:00 P.M. on Thursday, the house went dry. After six days and five nights, the bizarre condensation visitation stopped, never to return. Naturally the Frederick family was thrilled. And their insurance company was ecstatic. Because the reason for the water invasion was never located or explained, it refused to pay a dime in damages.

THE RUNAWAY RETENTION POND

In the blink of an eye, waterfront homeowners watch their greatest natural asset go down the drain.

In the residential real estate business, few amenities are as hard to resist, or as hard to obtain, as lakefront property. In the town of Wildwood, Missouri, an upscale St. Louis suburb, this valuable geographic blessing was enjoyed by the people nestled around twenty-three-acre (9.3 hectare) Lake Chesterfield, a glistening bit of water encircled by more than 670 condos and houses. But in June 2004, the God of Property Values sprang a nasty surprise. After weeks of heavy rains had swelled the lake, the water level suddenly began falling. And falling. On Monday the decline was barely noticeable. But by Wednesday the human-made pond, which in its heyday was ten feet (3 m) deep in spots, was gone. In the blink of an eye, it had drained like a bathtub.

To say the residents were surprised is putting it mildly. "It's disheartening, getting out on your deck and seeing this," George English, proud owner of a formerly waterfront condo, told the Associated Press. "One day it's a beautiful lake, and now, bingo, it's gone."

What it left behind was decidedly less pleasing: A sprawling, oozing mud flat littered with the stinking carcasses of dead fish. At least there was no mystery as to how it happened. When geologists inspected the lakebed, they found that the water it formerly contained had eroded the limestone beneath it, creating a vast sinkhole. When the erosion finally ate its way up to the lake, the water emptied into the void beneath.

Stopping up the hole was, as one would imagine, difficult, time-consuming, and expensive. And since the lake was located on private property, the Lake Chesterfield homeowners association had to foot most of the six-figure bill itself. But finally, in March 2005, the sink-hole was successfully plugged and the lake refilled. The problem, of course, is that this is a place where nature obviously never intended a body of water to be. Which explains why, in September 2005, the lake popped *another* leak and once more started to drain. Still, the area's homeowners, who each chipped in about $1,000 to restore their liquid asset, have little choice but to keep fighting. Owning a slice of prime pit-front property just doesn't have much of a ring to it.

Not-so-beautiful Lake Chesterfield, after nature pulled the cork.

HANGING BY A THREAD

There's a thin line between the normal and the strange. Some people have actually seen it.

The Essex County, New Jersey, suburb of Caldwell is the sort of neat, well-ordered place where strange things almost never happen. Almost. But when, once in a blue moon, something odd does occur, it's a doozy.

Just ask Mr. and Mrs. A. P. Smith of 85 Forest Street. On August 2, 1970, the couple noticed a glistening silver thread hanging over the home. It wasn't something pedestrian, like a length of kite string that had been caught in a tree. The strand, according to numerous witnesses, seemed to descend from a clear sky. And try as they might, no one could see exactly what the line was attached to—even with the aid of binoculars. It simply went up and up into the great unknown until it vanished from sight.

The strand hung around, literally, for about a month, as did a similar filament suspended more or less over a backyard pool on nearby Hillside Street. They didn't go straight up into the sky, but rather ascended at thirty- to fifty-degree angles. They could be pulled down, and they seemed to have a tensile strength comparable to two-pound (1 kg) test fishing line. Strangely enough, the strand seemed taut, as if whatever held the other end was pulling ever so slightly. Over the course of the visitation, neighborhood kids hauled in great quantities of the stuff, which seemed to be hollow and similar to nylon.

No matter how much was pulled down, however, there always seemed to be plenty more. Both of the sky lines persisted through fair weather and foul, until finally, one day, they inexplicably grew slack, then went away. No one ever saw them again. And no one ever figured out what they were, either—in spite of the fact that a sample was allegedly analyzed by the DuPont company. Lab tests reportedly showed that the stuff resembled nylon, but wasn't.

Which left an even more unsettling mystery to contemplate. What had been keeping it up there? Or, more to the point, who or what had been holding the other end?

HO, SWEET HO

Sneaking the world's oldest profession into suburbia is a pretty neat trick.

The folks in the upscale McKinney, Texas, neighborhood of Huntington Court probably felt a bit uneasy when their new neighbor, a U.S. Virgin Islands–born Canadian citizen named Conrad "T-Bone" Hendrickson, set up house in 1993. After all, guys with nicknames like "T-Bone" are usually found at biker bars and tattoo parlors, not holed up in a large family home on a quiet cul-de-sac. Many figured he was up to no good.

And they figured right. By the time the police took him away, the locals had seen every one of their fears proved correct. In a neighborhood more accustomed to school buses and backyard barbecues, Hendrickson hosted clothing-optional pool parties; entertained legions of visitors after hours (way after hours); and choked the street with the cars owned by his endless stream of guests. His lawn was also the scene of regular arguments and low-grade confrontations, some of which had to be broken up by police.

All this mayhem was fallout from Hendrickson's home-based business. His profession, as it turned out, was the oldest profession. The trophy sitting on his fireplace mantel said it all. It was given to him by one of his employees, and read "#1 Pimp of the Year, 1998."

And by "pimp" the trophy giver didn't mean "someone who lives a garish, expensive lifestyle." She meant that suburban homeowner T-Bone Hendrickson was also an honest-to-goodness, high-living, bling-wearing whorehouse proprietor. Authorities say that, when federal agents finally shut him down, Hendrickson was keeping a stable of some twenty prostitutes who operated mostly out of his $200,000 home. He was making hundreds of thousands of dollars—as were his girls, many of whom were so flush with cash that they started buying investment properties in the area.

At first glance, the idea of a whorehouse in the 'burbs seems strange—but only at first glance. Vice, like everything else, goes where the money is. Just as convenience stores and gas stations spring up next to new housing developments, so do groups and individuals who cater to less-savory human needs.

Plus, the suburbs are a nice place for the upwardly mobile pimp and ho to buy a house, put down roots, turn a few tricks, and save for the future. The advantages are obvious. The clientele enjoys the convenience of getting their rocks off nearby, as opposed to piling into the family SUV and cruising scary neighborhoods in search of action. And the pros love it because they're working (pardon the pun) virgin territory—small towns policed by a clueless constabulary more accustomed to dealing with petty vandalism and fender benders than hardcore vice.

Of course, the rules of suburban hooking are different. One can't just put on a miniskirt and a pair of fishnet stockings and loiter under the nearest streetlamp. Business is usually conducted via cellular phone or the Internet. Trysts can take place at the location of the john's choosing or, as in Hendrickson's case, at his house. Police say T-Bone had been working in his chosen field for more than a decade before heading for the suburbs and buying his piece of the American dream. Incredibly, he and his girls reportedly shared an almost Horatio Alger—like faith in the concept of self-improvement. The plan, almost universally shared by everyone on his staff, was to work hard, invest their money, and retire wealthy.

About the only people who didn't buy into this scheme were Hendrickson's neighbors. Fed up with the bare-breasted beauties who could regularly be seen frolicking in his backyard, they let federal agents use their upstairs bedrooms as surveillance centers. Slowly the cops gathered up enough incriminating pictures and videotape to shut Hendrickson down and seize his assets. However, 1998's #1 Pimp of the Year eluded them. He fled to Canada, only to be apprehended by the Canadian Mounties and returned to Texas for trial.

Hendrickson got busted because he violated a cardinal rule of happy suburban living: Don't tick off your neighbors. But he wasn't the only pimp to set up shop in the hinterlands. Similar operations have turned up everywhere from New Jersey to Atlanta to Redondo Beach, California. In most cases, the operators kept a much lower profile than T-Bone did—which meant the neighbors were doubly surprised when the paddy wagons arrived. "It just goes to show you," McKinney police chief Doug Kowalski told local Texas TV station CBS 11. "Never judge a person by the exterior of his house."

THE UFO IN THE ATTIC

A Florida town turns into a hot spot for flying saucers and odd encounters. Or perhaps not.

The seaside community of Gulf Breeze, Florida, is unique in a number of ways. Located just a short ride from nearby Pensacola, this hamlet is surrounded by a phalanx of United States military facilities, from Elgin Air Force Base to the east to Pensacola Naval Air Station to the west. Day and night, military aircraft of almost every description skirt the town's perimeter.

But that's not what made this place famous. Starting in the late 1980s, Gulf Breeze garnered worldwide headlines for hosting flying objects of the unidentified kind. For several years the town was supposedly the site of an extraterrestrial air show so intense, and so well documented, that more than a few "experts" considered the activity to be proof positive of alien visitation.

The story began in 1987 with local building contractor Edward

Walters. He asserted that while working late on the evening of November 11, a strange light appeared outside the window of his house. Heading outdoors, he said he encountered a hovering UFO that was shaped like a top, studded with portholes and sporting a luminous ring around its base. Walters grabbed a camera from his house, took several pictures from his yard, then stepped out into the street for a better angle. Suddenly the UFO lurched forward, hovered directly over him, and zapped him with a bright blue beam of light. The ray lifted him off the ground and stunned him. A voice in his head said, "Don't worry, we will not harm you." Then he blacked out. When he awakened, the spacecraft was gone.

About a week later, Walters took the photos to the *Gulf Breeze Sentinel*, along with a complete description of the "blue light" incident. Yet, for some reason, he didn't own up to the shots, saying instead that they were given to him by a "Mr. X." The *Sentinel* reported the story, and the media rush was on.

UFO enthusiasts from around the country descended on the area. The Mutual UFO Network (MUFON) even provided Walters (who eventually confessed that he took the pictures) with a special camera to use should he encounter more aliens. And wouldn't you know it, he did. With the help of the new equipment, he was able to provide even better shots of the strange, otherworldly craft.

Soon more locals got into the act. A man named Arthur Hufford stated that he and his wife saw a UFO hovering above some trees in nearby Pensacola. Eventually a small army of witnesses came forward, claiming to have encountered strange lights. In all, more than two hundred reports have been filed since Walters went public with his story in 1987. The Gulf Breeze UFOs became so commonplace that many people took to standing on the beach at night waiting for lights to appear. And, amazingly, they often weren't disappointed.

All of which makes what happened next so baffling. Walters became such a celebrity that visitors and the media ringed his home at 612 Silverthorn Road. So he sold the place and moved to a new, less-accessible residence. His old house was purchased by Robert E.

Menzer, who, while fiddling with an attic water line so that he could install an ice maker, made a fascinating discovery. When he pushed aside some foam insulation, he found a nine-inch (23 cm) long, five-inch (12 cm) deep model of a UFO built out of several glued-together foam picnic plates, a sheet of blue plastic film, an orange paper ring, and a couple of other doodads.

None of the pieces, it goes without saying, was of extraterrestrial origin.

The *Pensacola News Journal* broke the news of this latest "sighting" on June 10, 1990. Walters, who clung to his story with the tenacity of a bulldog (perhaps because he was negotiating everything from a book deal to a TV miniseries), claimed that "only a fool would leave behind such a piece of evidence." He went on to claim that the ersatz UFO was a plant, put there by someone seeking to discredit him.

This version of events struck a certain chord with a portion of the UFO and conspiracy communities. But for most of Gulf Breeze, the jig was up. The plot got even thicker when a Pensacola teenager reported that he helped Walters rig the photos. Originally, he was also supposed to take the shots to the local newspapers, claim them as his own, and pass himself off as a corroborating witness to Walters's original "close encounter." But though the kid balked at taking responsibility for the pictures, he claimed he did help fake a UFO landing site by turning over a trampoline and jumping on it to flatten the grass. As a crowning indignity, the *News Journal* even used the little model they obtained from Menzer to make their own "UFO photos," which were indistinguishable from the ones Walters produced. In short order, the only remaining mystery was how so many people could be so easily duped by such a low-tech farce. And, perhaps, why Walters didn't take his flying saucer model with him when he moved, instead of ditching it in his attic.

And that, as they say, was that. Or at least it should have been. The strange thing is that while the most famous Gulf Breeze sightings were thoroughly discredited, a segment of the UFO community didn't seem to get the memo. The Internet is still filled with breathless stories of the encounters, many of which pooh-pooh the testimony of the teenager who says he helped Walters. They also, in true conspiracy-nut fashion, expound at great length on claims that the model in the attic was created by a person or persons unknown in order to cast doubt on the entire affair. Apparently, some folks are buying into this. Even now, just as at the height of the flying saucer frenzy more than a decade ago, people still line up on the beaches after dark to catch a glimpse of strange, floating lights.

What's really creepy is that they keep seeing them. No one's produced a set of photos as stunning as the ones created by Walters, but plenty of people have shot or videotaped dancing lights in the darkness, out beyond the surfline. Are they UFOs, jets from the nearby military bases, or hoaxers tying road flares to small balloons? It could be any of those—or all three. All that can be said with certainty is that, after the dustup over Walters and his dodgy photographs, separating fiction from reality is almost impossible.

THE RING

San Luis Obispo, California, situated about an hour up the coast from Los Angeles, is an idyllic spot that reminds one of how the Golden State used to be, before all the people, gridlock, and smog arrived. Few things disturb the good vibes—except, perhaps, for the strange phone calls. Whoever places them doesn't say anything annoying, like asking if your refrigerator is running. In fact, he says nothing at all.

Instead of using a medium or Ouija board to communicate with the living, some ghosts just pick up a phone.

But that's what makes it so unnerving. Because if local legend is correct, the calls come from the worrywart manager of a local hotel—a manager who died more than half a century ago.

Fortunately, the phantom caller usually confines his pranks to his former place of employ, the palatial Paso Robles Inn. First opened in 1891 as El Paso de Robles Hotel, it was (and still is) famous for its hot springs baths and spa. But tragedy struck in 1940, when the building caught fire and nearly burned to the ground. The death toll could have been horrific were it not for night clerk J. H. Emsley. He spotted the blaze and raised the alarm, allowing everyone to escape. Everybody but himself. Shortly after Emsley got the word out, he dropped dead from a heart attack.

But although his life ended that night, his concern for the hotel and its inhabitants seems as keen as ever.

The structure was rebuilt using bricks from the original edifice and was renamed the Paso Robles Inn. But in recent times, the front desk has started receiving peculiar phone calls from room 1007. Whenever the clerk picks up that line, no one's there. And when staffers have been dispatched to see what the problem might be, they find the room vacant. Phone company personnel inspected both the inside and out-side connections but could find nothing amiss.

The calls, if they had only been placed to the front desk, probably wouldn't have attracted much attention. But then, on February 1, 2004, the phantom caller dialed 911. "That's not a glitch," general manager Paul Wallace told the *Seattle Times*. "That's not someone [just] dialing 0."

That's also not something the police and emergency services people take lightly. But there was no one to blame but the ghost. The evening of the 911 call, the hotel's head of maintenance, Mike Childs, visited the room to personally check the phone. While there, he actually saw it light up on its own and put in a call to the front desk. But when he picked up the handset and tried to do the same thing himself, the phone cut him off, then used the room's second line to call the desk again. Reportedly, all the desk clerk heard when she accepted the call was an earful of peculiar-sounding static. "It [was] an odd kind of sound that she hadn't heard before," Childs told the *Seattle Times*. "It's bizarre."

Interestingly, the calls started shortly after the renovation and reopen-ing of the hotel's grand ballroom, which was the only bit of the old hotel to survive the fire that, indirectly, was responsible for the death of Emsley. Perhaps he's still hanging around, making sure that everything's in good shape. If so, then the guests can rest easy, knowing they're pro-tected by a smoke detector whose batteries will never run down.

FLY AWAY HOME

People who run airports hate it when unusual and unexpected things happen. That's why they got so irritated when Deke Slayton buzzed John Wayne Airport in a noisy, high-powered aerobatic plane back on the morning of June 13, 1993.

The authorities certainly had a right to be angry. After all, John Wayne Airport is a busy place, with more than nine million travelers arriving and departing in 2004 alone. It gets so much traffic because it serves not a particular city, but the vast area of suburban outposts dotting Orange County, California, just south of Los Angeles. If you live in Costa Mesa or Irvine or Newport Beach or Santa Ana or any of a dozen other sun-kissed spots, then John Wayne is where you go to avoid the crush and bother of LAX.

In addition, legions of well-heeled private pilots keep their planes

A veteran pilot takes off for a place that's beyond the reach of even the Federal Aviation Administration.

there. On the morning of June 13, at 7:57 A.M., a powerful Formula One racing plane took off and performed stunt after aerobatic stunt within sight of the airport. The machine was fitted out with an extremely loud high-speed propeller, and the noise quickly got on the nerves of ground personnel. Many of them, aeronautics professionals and trained observers, made a point of writing down the Federal Aviation Administration–mandated registration code that was painted on the plane's side in huge, impossible-to-miss numbers and letters—N21X. After the hotdogging pilot finally left the area, they duly reported the incident to the FAA, which issued a letter of citation against the flyer assigned those numbers.

Because the gears of bureaucracy grind slowly, the letter didn't go out until June 28, and it didn't find its way into the appropriate hands until July 20. The hands in question were those of Bobbie Slayton, wife of astronaut Donald K. "Deke" Slayton. He was one of the original seven Mercury astronauts, the captain of the 1975 Apollo-Soyuz mission, and an avid racing plane pilot. The plane did, in fact, belong to her husband. But that didn't stop her from calling the FAA, asking if they'd lost their minds.

The simple fact was, Deke Slayton hadn't been anywhere near John Wayne Airport at the time listed on the citation. He'd died of brain cancer six hours earlier, in Texas, in the presence of Bobbie and their daughter, Stacey. Her husband was indeed the owner of N21X, but at the time of the sighting it was gathering dust in an aircraft museum in Sparks, Nevada, northeast of San Francisco. Its noisy engine, which had caused so much consternation at the airport that morning, had been pulled from the aircraft and sat forlornly beside it.

Not surprisingly, an investigation ensued. But not the usual ghost-hunting spectacle involving quests for "cold spots" and psychics casting about for spirit presences. Local authorities launched a swift, no-nonsense query into who, or what, had violated the Orange County Codified Ordinance, Section 2-1-30. But the information they gathered only made things more confusing—unless you accepted the idea that a plane and a pilot who couldn't possibly have been airborne that day *had* been airborne.

Its appearance had been anything but ghostlike. During the plane's maneuvers it sent three airport-area noise monitors well above acceptable levels. Likewise, ground witnesses doggedly stuck to their story. The vehicle they saw was a bright red Formula One bearing the ID letters N21X.

There was one final oddity. Controllers indicated that the plane took off on its own, without assistance from ground personnel. But that was impossible. Deke Slayton's plane lacked an electrical starter, which meant that, to get it going, someone had to manually crank the propeller while the pilot jiggered the controls until the engine fired. Bobbie, who had come around to the idea that something fantastic had taken place, mused that perhaps her husband's best friend, Gus Grissom (who had died years earlier when Apollo 1 burned up on its launchpad) served as Deke's ground crew.

In spite of a careful review of the facts, the officials at John Wayne Airport and the FAA never figured out what happened. Of course, the logical thing to do would have been to wait for the pilot to land, and then question him. But that was the problem. Whoever flew the ghost of N21X that day didn't come back. Ground observers reported that, after performing some stunts within sight of the airport, the big red plane simply headed west and climbed. It disappeared into the heavens, never to be seen again.

PHOTO CREDITS